LEGENDS OF WARFARE

GROUND

Sd.Kfz.251

German Armored Half-Track in World War II

Schiffer Military History
4880 Lower Valley Road
Atglen, PA 19310

DAVID DOYLE

Other Schiffer books by the author

German Heavy Armored Cars: Sd.Kfz. 231, 232, 233, 263, and 234 in World War II,
978-0-7643-6649-9

Hummel and Nashorn/Hornisse: German Self-Propelled Artillery in World War II,
978-0-7643-5940-8

Panzerkampfwagen IV: The Backbone of Germany's WWII Tank Forces,
978-0-7643-5359-8

Library of Congress Control Number: 2026932955

Designed by Alexa Harris
Type set in Impact / Univers Lt STD / Minion Pro

ISBN: 978-0-7643-7159-2
ePub: 978-1-5073-0721-2
Printed in India
10 9 8 7 6 5 4 3 2 1

MIX Paper | Supporting responsible forestry FSC™ C016779

Published by Schiffer Publishing, Ltd.
4880 Lower Valley Road
Atglen, PA 19310
Phone: (610) 593-1777; Fax: (610) 593-2002
Email: Info@schifferbooks.com
Web: www.schifferbooks.com

Acknowledgments

It would not have been possible to create this book without the considerable and invaluable assistance of a number of friends and colleagues. Among them are Tom Kailbourn, Thomas Anderson, David Fletcher, Charles Kliment, Pat Stansell, Scott Taylor, Rick Forys, Bob Graebe, the late Walter Spielberger, and the late Don Moriarty. Most of all, I am indebted to my wonderful wife, Denise, not only for her hard work scanning many of these photos but also for her unflagging support.

All wartime photos not otherwise credited are from the US National Archives; all post–World War II photos not otherwise credited are by the author.

Contents

Introduction

French engineer Adolphe Kégresse is widely considered to be the father of the half-track. In 1911, Kégresse was employed by Czar Nicholas II both as his driver and to improve the mobility of the czar's autos.

Vehicles operating in snow and mud are hindered by a number of factors, but two of the major factors are traction and flotation. Flotation refers to ability of the vehicle to operate over the surface being traversed, rather than sinking into it. Flotation is improved by lowering the ground pressure exerted by the vehicle. This can be done either by reducing the weight of the vehicle, or by increasing the area of contact with the ground. Kégresse realized that rather than merely increasing the size, and thus the contact area, of the tires, a radical change in ground pressure could be brought about by using tracks and associated elongated rear suspension in lieu of the rear wheels.

The concept caught the attention of militaries worldwide. Canadian efforts in the 1930s, led by Joseph-Armand Bombardier, produced a vehicle with superior performance in the snow. US efforts yielded vehicles with powered front axles, which gave them better off-road performance than the half-tracks of other nations.

The German military, however, produced a broader range of half-track vehicles by size than any other nation—and, with over 15,000 produced, the most abundant of the German half-tracks is the subject of this volume, the *Sonderkraftfahrzeug* (special-purpose vehicle) 251.

This vehicle, developed by Adolphe Kégresse and photographed at the imperial garage of Czar Nicholas II, was one of the first half-track vehicles ever produced. It was intended for use over snow, as were many early half-tracks, and skis have been fitted to the front suspension.

Joseph-Armand Bombardier built upon Kégresse's notions when developing this machine, which he referred to as a snowmobile. Its half-track-like appearance is apparent.

With their driven front axle, American half-tracks were arguably the most-off-road-capable half-tracks fielded during World War II by any nation. The M3, as shown here in Sicily in June 1943, was the armored personnel carrier variant of the series. *National Archives*

German half-tracks did not have the powered front axles favored by the US, but their track runs relative to the overall length of the vehicles were considerably longer. Germany also fielded the broadest range of half-tracks, with this, the *Kettenkraftrad*, being the smallest of the range. *Patton Museum*

At the opposite end of the spectrum from the *Kettenkraftrad* was the massive 18-ton Sd.Kfz. 9, an unarmored half-track that in addition to serving as a prime mover was used as a recovery vehicle for tanks. *Patton Museum*

The Sd.Kfz. 11 3-ton half-track was built as a prime mover, primarily for medium field guns. For the most part, two types of unarmored bodies were mounted on these vehicles. The artillery body had seating for six, and a stowage compartment for ammunition behind the driver. The engineer body had three bench seats for transporting personnel. *Patton Museum*

CHAPTER 1

The A, B, C (and Ds) of the Sd.Kfz. 251

The medium *Schützenpanzerwagen*, or armored personnel carrier, was based on the chassis of the Sd.Kfz. 11 3-ton half-track and would form the backbone of Germany's armored infantry operations during World War II. Postwar Allied intelligence reports included a remark from General Heinz Guderian stating that the vehicles were "the greatest saver of blood we possess."

The chassis for the vehicles, HL.Kl.6p, were built first by Borgward and then later by Hanomag. As mentioned, these were based on the Sd.Kfz. 11 chassis and utilized the same clutch, four-speed transmission, suspension, and track. The engines differed between the armored and unarmored vehicles, the armored-vehicle engines (model HL 42 TUKRM) including an additional drive for the separately mounted cooling fan.

As compared to the Sd.Kfz. 11, the steering mechanism of the Sd.Kfz. 251 differed, with the steering wheel reverse-sloped at a 45-degree angle to the driver. The armored body was fabricated separately and mounted on the chassis, much like a conventional automobile body and chassis are joined together, as opposed to having a unibody like the Sd.Kfz. 234.

The forward portion of the body, which ended just behind the driver, protected the driver, commander, and engine. The rear section encompassed the open-topped area, initially designed to transport ten soldiers. An internal flange facilitated the bolting together of the two body sections. Deutsche Edelstahlwerke in Hannover initially produced the bodies for the Sd.Kfz. 251.

The initial production vehicle, designated Sd.Kfz. 251 Ausf. A, can be distinguished by the two vision slits, each with glass blocks and protected by an armored flap, in each side of the rear personnel compartment's 8 mm armor. This is a feature not found on successive models of the Sd.Kfz. 251.

Production of the Sd.Kfz. 251 began in May 1939, and the vehicles were used in limited numbers during Germany's invasion of Poland. About 232 Sd.Kfz. 251 Ausf. A are believed to have been built before production switched to the Sd.Kfz. 251 Ausf. B.

The Sd.Kfz. 251 Ausf. B. differed from the Ausf. A only in details, chief of which was the omission of the side vision slits in the rear body. A shortage of these vision slits was noted as being the cause of Sd.Kfz. 251 production falling short of requirements for the month of September 1939.

The shortage of vision slits was not the only material problem impacting Sd.Kfz. 251 production in 1939. A shortage of armor plate with which to fabricate bodies led to the production of 305 *mittlerer ungepanzerter Mannsch*. Trsp. Kw. (Sd.Kfz. 251)—that is, Sd.Kfz. 251 with mild-steel bodies. These vehicles were produced from June through December 1939. Further production of the unarmored variant was contemplated, and orders were even placed, but in December 1939 the decision was made to instead construct Sd.Kfz. 11 by using the chassis planned for additional unarmored Sd.Kfz. 251s.

The internal stowage was rearranged slightly, the most significant of this being the relocation of the radio from behind the codriver's seat to in front of his seat. The front machine gun mount became a simple pivot type, and armored gun shields were provided for the guns. The radio antenna was relocated from the right front fender to a position closer to the radio itself. Evidence suggests that approximately 350 of the Ausf. B vehicles were assembled.

In January 1940 the Ausf. C entered production, and more manufacturers became involved in the production of these vehicles. F. Schichau-Werke in Elbing began doing final assembly, utilizing chassis produced by Hanomag. These were chassis beyond those upon which Hanomag were mounting the armored bodies in-house.

Also, Maschinenfabrik Niedersachsen-Hannover (MNH) was contracted to produce the chassis for the Sd.Kfz. 251. MNH would replace Borgward (Hansa-Lloyd und Goliath) in the production of 251 chassis, Borgward chassis instead being used for Sd.Kfz. 11.

To meet the demand for the vehicle, welded armored bodies were also ordered from Schoeller-Bleckmann Stahlwerke in Ternitz, with deliveries beginning in March 1940. Even with this production joining that of Deutsche Edelstahlwerke, additional bodies were required.

Accordingly, additional bodies were ordered from Bohemia Boehm-Leipa. Unable to weld armor plate, this firm used riveted construction to assemble the bodies.

By November 16, 1940, earlier nomenclature for the vehicle "mittlerer gepanzerter Mannschaftskraftwagen" had given way to "mittlerer Schützenpanzerwagen."

Beyond Hanomag and MNH, who did some of their own final assembly, and the previously mentioned F. Schichau AG, the firms of Gollnow und Sohn, Eisenwerk Weserhütte, and Wumag all mounted armored Sd.Kfz. 251 bodies on chassis produced by Hanomag or MNH.

While the change in manufacturers is not apparent, other than for some vehicles having riveted rather than welded bodies, the Sd.Kfz. 251 Ausf. C was readily distinguishable from other models. The most obvious change was in the front of the vehicle. Previously the front plate of the engine compartment had been made of two intersecting pieces of armor, but with the introduction of the Ausf. C, the front plate was a single piece of flat armor plate. Also, at the front of the vehicle, the front bumper used on earlier models was eliminated, with the Ausf. C having no bumper.

Whereas the Ausf. A and Ausf. B drew engine-cooling air down through a grille at the top front of the armored engine hood, such air was now drawn up behind the armor plate. Large boxlike structures were added to either side of the engine compartment. These were armored covers to protect the cooling-air exhausts. The fenders over the tracks were also changed. Previously flat, with the introduction of the Ausf. C these fenders were slightly upswept near the front.

Internally, changes included adding stowage lockers behind the troop seats. The front seats were redesigned so they folded down and were readily removable for maintenance purposes.

By December 1, 1942, Büssing-NAG had completed design work on a new body style for the Sd.Kfz. 251. Dubbed the Ausf. D, the new body entered production at Deutsche Edelstahlwerke, Krefeld, on May 18, 1943. Deutsche Edelstahlwerke, Steinmueller, began deliveries of the new bodies the following month. Bohemia Boehm-Leipa, Schoeller-Bleckmann/Ternitz, and Ferrum Kattowitz's Laurahütte plant near Auschwitz, Poland, as well as Poldi Huette in Czechoslovakia, joined in the production of Ausf. D bodies. In order to maintain production levels yet allow Hanomag to cease final assembly (while still producing chassis), F. Schichau GmbH, Maschinen u. Lokomotivwerk, Elbing, was contracted as an assembly plant, with the firm's initial delivery in November 1943. The sprawling Schichau complex in Elbing, which included a shipyard, had 18,000 workers in 1944—including a reported 2,000 that were in a subcamp of the Stutthof concentration camp. By February 1945 the Soviets had taken Elbing.

To make up for this loss, it was planned to transfer that production to Weserhütte und Wumag Waggonfarik, Goerlitz.

Chassis production was adjusted as well. MNH left Sd.Kfz. 251 production in March 1943 to concentrate instead on Panther tank production. The void was filled by Adlerwerke, which began deliveries that month, Auto Union, where initial Sd.Kfz. 251 deliveries began in May, and Skoda, which began production in July 1943.

As compared to the previous models, the body of the Ausf. D was easier, and presumably faster and cheaper, to produce. The rear of the vehicle was completely restyled, the complex clamshell doors previously used giving way to a simple flat plate set at an angle, with hinged doors providing access. Along the vehicle sides, integral stowage bins replaced the stowage boxes previously mounted on top of the fenders. These bins enclosed the entire

The first model of the Sd.Kfz. 251 was the Ausführung (abbreviated Ausf.) A. Characteristics of the Ausf. A, as seen on this vehicle, included a tubular front bumper, two-piece frontal plates on the body, a ventilation grille on the top of the front of the body, pioneer-tool stowage on the sides of the body toward the rear, and two fixed vision ports on the side of the body, in addition to the driver's and assistant driver's hinged side visors. Both armored bodies and unarmored bodies were built for the Sd.Kfz. 251 Ausf. A; this example has the armored body. *Walter J. Spielberger collection*

space between the top of the track guards and the armored body. The large air ducts on either side of the engine compartment introduced on the Ausf. C were eliminated.

The armament of the personnel carrier evolved as well. A January 27, 1944, directive replaced the previously used 7.92 mm MG 34 with 7.92 mm MG 42 machine guns. Inside, the equipment layout was much the same as it had been in the Ausf. C; however, wood replaced metal and leather in many applications.

That the Sd.Kfz. 251 was important to the German war machine is evidenced by the inclusion of the vehicle in the February 28, 1945, emergency production program of armored vehicles, which called for the vehicle to remain in production until April 1945.

In addition to the armored Sd.Kfz. 251 Ausf. A half-tracks manufactured in 1939, a total of 305 Sd.Kfz. 251s were built with unarmored bodies that year, due to a shortage of armor plate. Several of those vehicles, designated *ungepanzerte* (unarmored), are lined up here. The license plate of the first one is WH-58718. *Bundesarchiv*

One of the unarmored Sd.Kfz. 251s produced in 1939 is viewed from the left side. This model had two vision slits on small, flat panels to the rear of the driver's side visor; these panels were flush, or nearly so, with the body. *Bundesarchiv*

Except for the different styles of visors to the rear of the drivers' compartment, the *gepanzerte* (armored) Sd.Kfz. 251 Ausf. A and the *ungepanzerte* Sd.Kfz. 251 were virtually indistinguishable by their exterior appearances. What appears to be an *ungepanzerte* Sd.Kfz. 251 is being hoisted on a railroad flatcar. Clamps for pioneer tools are visible toward the rear of the body. Bows for supporting a canvas top are above the top of the body.

Troops pose in their Sd.Kfz. 251. Jutting from the front of the driver's side visor is a turn indicator. The muffler is set in an opening in the dip in the fender to the rear of the tires. On the fronts of the fenders are thin rods with white balls on the tops; these were for helping the driver to judge clearance when driving through tight spaces. *Thomas Anderson collection*

One of the principal roles of the Sd.Kfz. 251 was that of prime-mover of light-artillery pieces. This *ungepanzerte* Sd.Kfz. 251 is towing a 10.5 cm leFH 18 (*liechte feldhaubitze*: light field howitzer). The two visors in the personnel compartment to the rear of the cab of the unarmored Sd.Kfz. 251s can be readily distinguished from those of armored Sd.Kfz. 251s in that the vision slits of the former are toward the centers of the visors, while armored vehicles' vision slits were at the bottoms of the visors. *NARA*

During the invasion of Greece on April 17, 1941, an Sd.Kfz. 251 pauses while soldiers make adjustments to equipment. On the front of the fender is the tactical symbol for a towed howitzer; the insignia of the 2nd Panzer Division, in the shape of an inverted Y, with a vertical bar to the right of it; and the number 207.

German mechanized artillery, including an Sd.Kfz. 251 towing a 10.5 cm leFH 18 (*at the center*), cross the border into Lithuania near Kalvarija on June 22, 1941, the first day of Operation Barbarossa, the invasion of the USSR. A spare tire is atop the rear of the body.

An Sd.Kfz. 251 Ausf. A of the 25th Panzer Regiment pauses along a road in the USSR on June 27, 1941. The vehicle is towing a trailer with two fuel drums, from which the motorcycle apparently is about to be refueled.

In Sipka Pass, Bulgaria, on April 3, 1941, an Sd.Kfz. 251 Ausf. A tows a 10.5 cm leFH 18. The bundle of stakes on the front of the vehicle is available for tossing into ditches to help vehicles negotiate them when necessary.

An unarmored Sd.Kfz. 251 drawing a 10.5 cm leFH 18 crosses an engineer bridge adjacent to a blown bridge. The ventilation doors at the front of the body and on the side of the engine compartment are secured in the open positions. *Thomas Anderson collection*

Coming ashore from a pontoon bridge is an unarmored Sd.Kfz. 251 laden with troops. Following is another Sd.Kfz. 251. A *Balkenkreuz* (Balkan cross) is marked in white on the frontal plate of the driver's compartment; additional ones are on the hull sides.

Sandbag protection has been added to the drivers' compartment roofs of the three Sd.Kfz. 251s in this view. On the left fender of the closest vehicle is the tactical symbol for motorized infantry; the "10" refers to the company number. Above the tactical symbol is the oak-leaf insignia of the 1st Panzer Division.

Although the Sd.Kfz. 251 had good off-road capability, when it encountered soft ground, the lack of front-wheel drive could prove to be a serious liability, as these soldiers working to recover the vehicle could attest. A German flag with swastika is draped over the hood, should any friendly aircraft be tempted to attack the disabled half-track. Of interest is the presence of shields for both the front and the rear machine guns.

A 10.5 cm leFH 18 is hitched to an unarmored Sd.Kfz. 251 assigned to the 78th Motorized Artillery Regiment of the 7th Panzer Division. A tarpaulin bow is installed near the rear of the body, and a full complement of pioneer tools is on the side of the body. *Thomas Anderson collection*

The crew of an unarmored Sd.Kfz. 251 pause to relax. The tactical symbol for the third battery of a motorized howitzer unit is on the front of the right fender. Farther to the rear on that fender, to the front of the stowage compartments, is a fire extinguisher. A fairly good view of the grille on the front of the hood is available.

An Sd.Kfz. 251 Ausf. A proceeds through a war-ravaged town 34 miles from Paris on June 17, 1940. A tarpaulin is rolled back on the upper rear of the body; faintly visible above the tarpaulin are the treads of a spare tire that is stowed on the upper rear of the body.

A column of Sd.Kfz. 251s with an Ausf. A in the lead advances through a settlement in the USSR or eastern Europe. The lead vehicle bears Wehrmacht license number WH-95709. On the left fender is the tactical sign for motorized infantry company number 3. Note the ditching stakes on the lead half-track and the spare tire on the front of the third vehicle. *Patton Museum*

The same Sd.Kfz. 251 Ausf. A seen in the foreground of the preceding photo is shown on a steppe with several other Sd.Kfz. 251s. Covers have been placed over the headlights of the nearest half-track, and on the side of the body is what appears to be a light-duty tow cable. *Patton Museum*

About to ford a stream, this Sd.Kfz. 251 is recognizable as an Ausf. A by the prominent visors on the side of the body. A blackout cover with a small slot on it is on the right headlight, while the left headlight lacks a cover. A tactical sign for motorized infantry with a large number "2" to the right of it is on the left fender. *Patton Museum*

A gunner in an Sd.Kfz. 251 has the MG 34 7.92 mm machine gun trained on an embankment adjacent to a destroyed railroad bridge. Above the assistant driver's side visor is an unusual feature: a plate fastened to the top of the body, with a tie-down loop at its lower rear corner. This may have been an improvised splash shield that continued around the front of the cab roof. *Patton Museum*

During Operation Barbarossa in 1941, an Sd.Kfz. 251 Ausf. A emerges from the water after crossing a stream. On the left fender is the inverted Y insignia used by the 1st Panzer Division during the invasion of the USSR. A bundle of stakes for use in crossing ditches is lashed to the front end.

An Sd.Kfz. 251 Ausf. A surmounts an embankment after crossing an engineer bridge during the invasion of Greece in 1941. Marked on the edge of the fender is the recommended tire pressure, 2.75 atü (a measure of air pressure used by the Germans: 1 atü is equal to 1 technical atmosphere). Early on, the radio antenna on the medium *Schützenpanzer* was mounted as seen here, on the dip in the right fender. Subsequently, the antenna was moved to a mount on the top of the body along the personnel compartment.

Wehrmacht troops are gathered on and around a well-worn Sd.Kfz. 251 Ausf. A (it is identifiable as such because one of the personnel-compartment visors is visible between the heads of the men standing at the left and at the center). The front fenders have been removed, the access flap for the engine-starting crank is missing, and the front bumpers and the turn indicators are no longer present. *Thomas Anderson collection*

The Sd.Kfz. 251 Ausf. B was virtually identical to the Sd.Kfz. 251 Ausf. A, except the Ausf. B lacked the two visors on each side of the body to the rear of the driver's and the assistant driver's side visors. Like the Ausf. A, the Ausf. B had provisions for storing pioneer tools on the side of the body.

Troops peer at the photographer from the interior of an Sd.Kfz. 251 Ausf. B. Faintly visible on the left rear door is a tactical symbol for a 9th Company armored infantry vehicle, below which is the "X" divisional symbol of the 5th Panzer Division. Below the doors is the tow pintle. A pick is stored on the side of the body.

An Sd.Kfz. 251 Ausf. B with ditching stakes and a spare tire secured to the front end is attempting to recover a Panhard Type 178 armored car that has become mired. Mats have been laid on the ground in front of the armored car to assist it once it becomes unstuck. On the left fender of the Panhard is the fish-shaped insignia of the 35th Infantry Division, which likely was the division the Sd.Kfz. 251 Ausf. B was assigned to. *Patton Museum*

This Sd.Kfz. 251 Ausf. B was assigned to the 9th Panzer Division in 1941. A small number "44" is marked on the plate to the front of the assistant driver's position. The forward machine gun mount is fitted with a shield formed from a bent armor plate with a slot for the machine gun barrel up the center. On the roof of the cab to the front of the machine gun mount is a curved splash guard, to keep bullets and splinters from ricocheting into the personnel compartment. A section of spare track is draped over the front of the hood. *Walter J. Spielberger collection*

In a photo likely taken at the same place and time as the preceding one, two Sd.Kfz. 251 Ausf. Bs negotiate a rough trail. The second vehicle is the same one in the preceding image. The closer half-track has a roll of wire stowed on the front end. Very faintly visible on the right fender is the insignia of the 9th Panzer Division: the letter *Y* with two horizontal bars to the right of it. On the left fender is a large letter *K* and a tactical sign for an engineer unit, third company. A small number "43" is marked outboard of the assistant driver's visor. *Patton Museum*

On a road leading to Martelange, Luxembourg, on November 5, 1940, an Sd.Kfz. 251, likely an Ausf. B, passes a column of vehicles. Two tiers of sandbags are piled on the cab roof, and a piece of fabric, likely a German flag or recognition panel, is lashed over the hood. *National Archives*

In a photo taken on the same road and the same date as the preceding one, an Sd.Kfz. 251 Ausf. B passes by. The structure over the cab roof is a map table or platform with a wind deflector to the front and sides, supported by legs. These tables were produced to a standard design and were retrofitted to a limited number of Ausf. A and Ausf. B vehicles for use by platoon leaders of armored infantry companies.

Another Sd.Kfz. 251 equipped with the map table with wind deflector. This vehicle is also equipped with what appears to be appliqué armor, which covers several of the stowage boxes on the fender. The presence of this armor makes it impossible to determine if the vehicle is equipped with visors in the rear compartment, characteristic of the Ausf. A, or if this is the more common Ausf. B. *BA 268-0167-27A*

In a photo taken on the eastern front on July 25, 1941, in the foreground is an Sd.Kfz. 251 Ausf. B, accompanying a half-track towing a howitzer. In the background are other half-tracks, including Sd.Kfz. 251s. The vehicle in the foreground has two shovels, a starter crank, and what appears to be a crowbar clamped to the side of the body.

Several soldiers pose around the open engine compartment of a camouflage-painted Sd.Kfz. 251 Ausf. B. at a training center. A placard that reads "*Fahrschule*" (Driving School) is on the front of the body above the license plate (WH-363028). A Notek blackout headlight is on the left fender next to the left service headlight. The front bumper is missing. *Thomas Anderson collection*

A column advancing along a road in a forest in the Soviet Union in October 1941 includes two Sd.Kfz. 251s and a Pz.Kpfw. II light tank. The closer Sd.Kfz. 251 is an Ausf. B, and both of the half-tracks have whitewash camouflage to make them blend in with the snowy terrain. A section of spare track is draped over the front of the hood.

The crew of an Sd.Kfz. 251 Ausf. B is wary for threats at the railroad station at Aiviekste, Latvia, in June 1941. This vehicle has a map platform over the cab. The *Balkenkreuz* on the rear of the vehicle is centered to the right of the joint separating the two doors. What appears to be a white border has been painted on the rear of the body to the sides and above the tops of the upper halves of the doors. *Thomas Anderson collection*

Several Sd.Kfz. 251s, including an Ausf. B in the foreground, are operating in a grassy field. Two MG 34s are ready for action in the nearest vehicle. The forward MG 34 was intended to engage targets on the ground. The rear MG 34 was on a swiveling mount called the *Fliegerschwenkarm*, designed to allow the machine gun to be used against both aerial and ground targets. In some cases, a *Fliegerschwenkarm* was mounted at the front and at the rear of the personnel compartment. *Thomas Anderson collection*

During the blitzkrieg through France, Wehrmacht troops make preparations for continuing the advance near Neuhabich on May 16, 1940. In the foreground are two Sd.Kfz. 251 Ausf. Bs with very prominent white tactical signs for motorized infantry, with the number 3 on the left fenders and large rolls of wire stowed on the front ends. Sandbags are piled on the cab roof of the second vehicle.

During the German invasion of Greece in 1941, an Sd.Kfz. 251 Ausf. B operates with two Pz.Kpfw. I tanks. A roll of wire is stowed on the front of the vehicle, and both machine gun mounts are equipped with armored shields. The fire extinguisher is absent from its holder on the fender.

The Sd.Kfz. 251 Ausf. C marked several noticeable changes in the body. The two-piece front of the body gave way to a single plate, tilted backward at the top. Armored shrouds were now included over the vents on the sides of the hood. The storage compartments on the side of the vehicle were moved to the rear. The pioneer tools were moved to the fenders. Here, brand-new Sd.Kfz. 251 Ausf. Cs are lined up at the Reichsgebiet, a vehicle depot in Berlin, sometime in 1942. *BA 811-2231-24*

Three Sd.Kfz. 251 Ausf. Cs assigned to the 24th Panzer Division are parked with other vehicles near a temporary bridge somewhere in the USSR during the 1941 invasion. The turn signals had been moved from their locations on the Ausf. A and B, to the front of the driver's and assistant driver's side visors, to the fenders to the rear of the new cowlings on the sides of the hood.

Early Sd.Kfz. 251 personnel carriers that were equipped with radios had the sets mounted on the right side of the personnel compartment, to the rear of the assistant driver's seat, as seen here. This location was difficult for the assistant driver to access, so later the radio was moved to the front of his station. Here, a crewman in an Sd.Kfz. 251 Ausf. C operates the *Funksprechgerat* (FuSpr) F, (radio set type F). The operator has a throat microphone set, with the send-receive control in his hand. Above the radio is a speaker, and above that is a guard for the radio. Above that guard is the antenna and its base.

The Sd.Kfz. 251 Ausf. C lacked the front bumper found on earlier models. The pioneer tool clamps and holders on the sides of the hull were no longer there. Also, the three storage containers on each side of the vehicle were moved almost to the rears of the fenders.

New Sd.Kfz. 251 Ausf. Cs are ready to leave a vehicular facility. The fire extinguisher formerly stored on the right fender on the Ausf. A and B now was located on the inside of the left rear door. Bows and in some cases tarpaulins are on the bodies above the personnel compartments, and on at least the nearest vehicle, a *Fliegerschwenkarm* antiaircraft machine gun mount is installed. *Walter J. Spielberger collection*

During the campaign in the Soviet Union in 1942, an Sd.Kfz. 251 Ausf. C, *foreground*, operates with a *leichte Funkpanzerwagen* (light armored radio carrier) based on the Sd.Kfz. 250. A faded white *Balkenkreuz* and the vehicle number "136" are on the side of the Sd.Kfz. 251. *BA 792-0138-21A*

Personnel, including one scanning the horizon with binoculars, are on the alert in an Sd.Kfz. 251 Ausf. C along the southern front in Russia in the late summer of 1942. Two jerry cans are secured to the front plate of the vehicle, and another jerry can is stowed toward the front of the right fender.

Occasionally an Sd.Kfz. 251 in good condition fell into the hands of Allied forces, such as this Ausf. C vehicle with a riveted body and a camouflage paint scheme, photographed at Aberdeen Proving Ground, Maryland, in late July 1943. "CAPTURED ENEMY MATERIEL" is painted along the top of the body, and a 1-foot ruler is leaning against the tire for dimensional reference. Note the rather flimsy stowage rack made of metal strapping on the side of the body. *Ordnance Museum*

The Sd.Kfz. 251 Ausf. C at Aberdeen Proving Ground is seen in a photo apparently taken well after the July 1942 photo. The paint finish on the vehicle is severely weathered. The two identification crosses on the body are still visible, but the markings identifying this as captured enemy materiel are barely visible. *Ordnance Museum*

The vehicle in the previous photo, although in operational condition when captured, was placed on exterior display at Aberdeen Proving Ground, where it deteriorated considerably. The vehicle was transferred to the Texas Military Forces Museum at Camp Mabry in Austin on February 26, 1993, where it was given an extensive cosmetic restoration.

The muffler was located in the well between the left front and rear fenders. The exhaust pipe enters the top of the muffler, and the exhaust outlet is the short, oval pipe on the side. The armored body of the Ausf. C incorporated a cowl jutting from each side of the engine compartment; the left one is at the top of the photo. These cowls enclosed the warm-air outlets. To the rear of the cowl is the left turn signal.

In a view of the left side of the Sd.Kfz. 251 Ausf. C are, *from left to right*, the left turn signal, the rear fender, the manual starter crank, and three storage boxes. Roundheaded rivets were used to assemble the armor plates.

The right idler, at the rear of the track suspension, and, *at right*, the rear bogie wheel are depicted. The idler wheels as well as the inner sets of bogie wheels had six reinforcing ribs on their surfaces. The outer bogie wheels had smooth surfaces. The idler and bogie wheels were equipped with solid rubber tires.

The Sd.Kfz. 251 Ausf. C sprockets, at the front of the track suspensions, had hubcaps with a flat surface and two notches on opposite sides. One notch is easily discerned on the top of the hubcap, while the other notch is on the bottom of the cap. The sprocket teeth were fitted with small rollers. Each track link has a rectangular rubber pad on it.

A left rear view of the Camp Mabry Sd.Kfz. 251 Ausf. C portrays the rivet patterns on the armored body. Below the dual doors on the rear of the body is the tow pintle. The dark-colored feature above the license plate on the rear of the left fender is a Notek convoy taillight.

The layout of the right side of the Sd.Kfz. 251 Ausf. C is similar to that of the left side, except there is no muffler on the right side. To the rear of the right side visor is a base mount for a radio antenna.

The sheet metal storage boxes above the rear fenders were secured to the armored body with brackets and hex screws. Each box has a vertical door with three leaf hinges on the bottom and two latches on top.

The turn signal, mounted on the armored body above the sprocket on each side of the vehicle, incorporated a vane inside a protective box. The vane swiveled out to indicate that the driver was making a turn.

The hubcaps of this Sd.Kfz. 251 Ausf. C are conical with flattened tips. The wheels were secured with eight hex screws. The tires were made of artificial rubber and were size 7.25-20.

In a view of the Camp Mabry Sd.Kfz. 251 Ausf. C from the front, in the foreground is the round armored cover for the radiator filler, to the rear of which are the two access doors for the engine, with two hinges per door. To the rear is the front of the driver's compartment, with the left cast-armor visor open. The vision slit is visible on the lower part of the right visor. Above the fighting compartment are a 7.92 mm MG 34 and three curved bows, to support a canvas cover for that compartment.

A front view of the vehicle shows the blackout covers over the service headlights. Below the license plate is the round cover for the socket for the manual starter crank. Also in view are the front tow hooks and part of the front suspension.

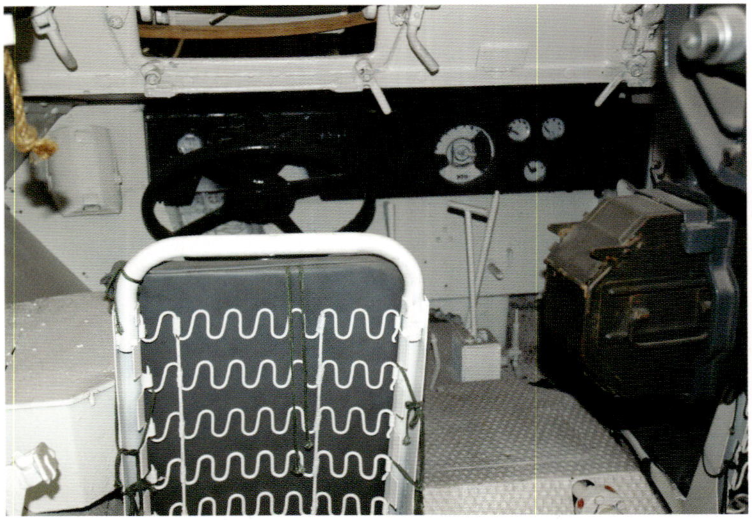

This is a view from behind the driver's seat, with its zigzag springs on a tubular metal frame. To the front of the seat is the tilted steering wheel. The large dial on the instrument panel is the tachometer. Above the wheel is the driver's front vision port. To the far right is a magazine for the 7.92 mm MG 34, in a holder on the lower part of the machine gun mount.

A radio set generally was mounted in the right side of the driver's compartment when the vehicle was assigned to a platoon leader. A seat was provided for him to the right of the driver's seat. At the top center and top right are, respectively, the platoon leader's visor and his right-side visor.

The MG 34 on the Camp Mabry Sd.Kfz. 251 Ausf. C is attached to an sMG Lafette (heavy machine gun carriage). The handwheel at the bottom operates a screw shaft to elevate and depress the machine gun. Suspended on a rod at the lower center is an ammunition magazine for the gun.

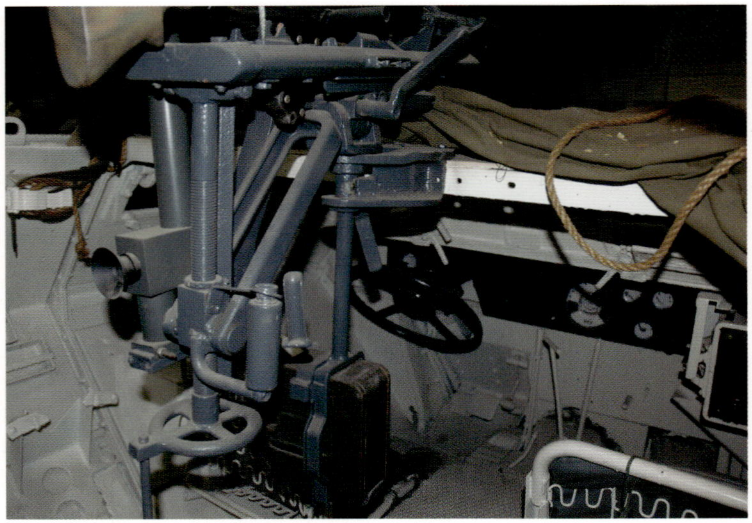

The sMG Lafette is viewed from the right rear, with the driver's compartment visible below and to the front. On the left side of the machine gun carriage is a periscopic sight with a conical eyepiece. Using the sight and the controls on the lower part of the gun carriage, the gunner could aim and fire the piece without exposing himself above the fighting compartment.

The periscopic sight is at the center, with the machine gun carriage and elevating screw next to it. Linked 7.92 mm rounds have been fed into the MG 34's chamber. The machine gun carriage is mounted on the bracket to the left, which is attached to the roof of the driver's compartment.

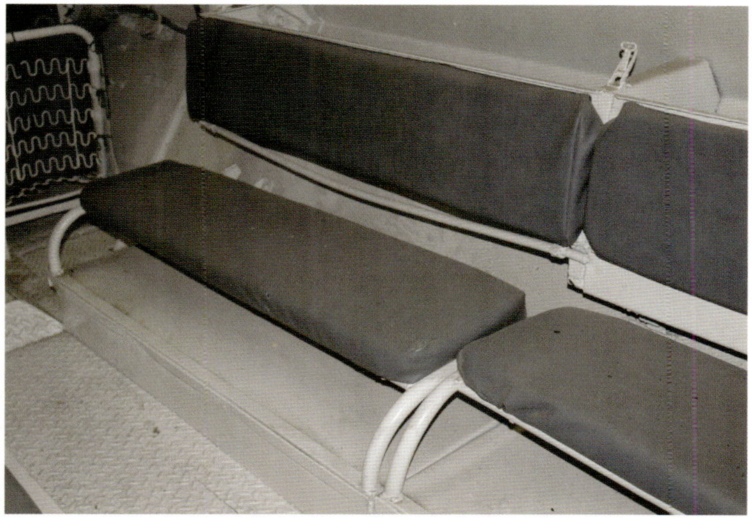

Bench seats to hold up to ten passengers are in the fighting compartment of the Sd.Kfz. 251 Ausf. C. These seats are on the right side. The seat bottoms are in two sections, on tubular frames, while the seat backs are attached to stowage bins on the inside of the armored body.

The seating in the fighting compartment is seen from the left rear corner of the compartment. To the upper left are rifle racks. The floor is of diamond-tread plate, with removable panels in it.

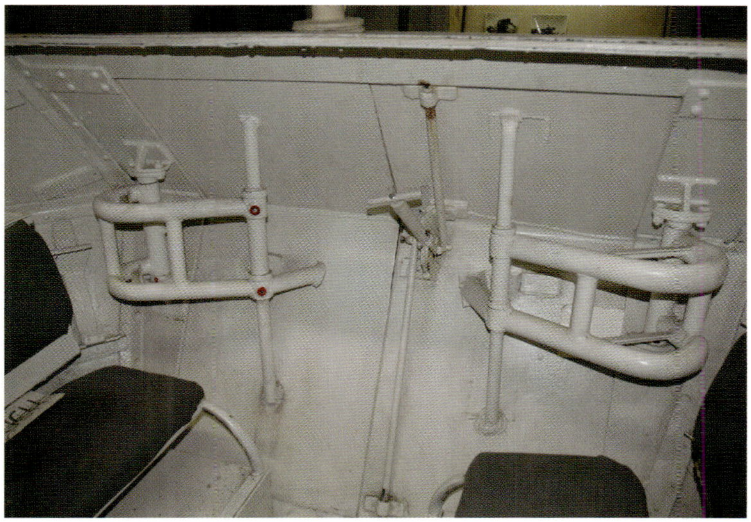

The rear doors of the Sd.Kfz. 251 Ausf. C have elaborate, heavy-duty hinge assemblies. On the inside of the left door (*on the right*) is the locking system for the doors.

With the doors on the hood open on a riveted-body Sd.Kfz. 251 Ausf. C, license WH01539986, the thickness of their armor as well as that of the hood is apparent. The top of the hood was 5 mm thick, while the frontal plates of the cab and the body (*right foreground*) were 14.5 mm thick. *Thomas Anderson collection*

An example of a riveted-body Sd.Kfz. 251 Ausf. C is depicted. It was very likely painted overall in *Dunkelgrau* (dark gray) RAL 7021, which was the principal camouflage color for German military vehicles from 1940 to 1943, when *Dunkelgelb* (dark yellow) replaced it. Bows for a tarpaulin cover are installed on the top of the body. Net to the front bow is a mount for a radio antenna.

"Panther" is the nickname painted on the ventilation cowl of this Sd.Kfz. 251/7 Ausf. C with the insignia of "Leibstandarte SS Adolf Hitler" on the right fender. The Sd.Kfz. 251/7 was a combat engineer half-track with brackets on the sides for carrying two portable treadway bridge sections called *Übergangsschienen*. Spare tracks are on the front and top of the hood. *Thomas Anderson collection*

On the steppes of the eastern front in the summertime, a soldier takes advantage of a pause in the action to disassemble an MG 34 for cleaning and maintenance. The gun barrel is on the hood to the front of the soldier's feet. A light color, probably dark yellow, has been sprayed over the vehicle and the gun shield to make the half-track blend in with the local terrain. *Thomas Anderson collection*

Two Sd.Kfz. 251s, including an Ausf. C in the foreground, are part of an advancing column. The sign in the foreground warns that there is a bridge ahead. Faintly visible on the lower part of the right rear door is the insignia of the 23rd Panzer Division, an angled arrow with a bar through the shaft, to the left of which is a rendering of the Eiffel Tower, which often accompanied the 23rd Panzer Division's insignia.

In the use for which it was designed, an Sd.Kfz. 251/1 Ausf. C laden with troops moves through a Russian town during the summer of 1942. Ammunition is visible in the feed to the machine gun; thus the area is presumably still considered hostile. The flat faces of the frontal armor, and slight upsweep of the track fenders as well as the rearward-mounted stowage compartments, all characteristics of this *Ausführung*, or model, are plainly visible. *BA 093-0008-23A*

Several officers are using this Sd.Kfz. 251 Ausf. C as a staff vehicle. Two radio antennas are present: one on the right side and one to the rear. The number "36" is painted under the driver's side visor. *Thomas Anderson collection*

Proceeding along on a dusty road are an Sd.Kfz. 251 Ausf. C and a cargo truck. The machine gun is dismounted from the front mount, and a tarpaulin is partially rigged over the personnel compartment. Spare track links are suspended from the front of the vehicle, and a spare bogie wheel is on the left fender.

Local camouflage in the form of tree branches is affixed to this Sd.Kfz. 251 Ausf. C. A section of spare track is stashed in the dip in the fender to the lower right. A name that, unfortunately, is illegible is painted on the body below the radio antenna, using a tone of paint that is only slightly darker than the body. Canteens and mess kits are hanging from the body to the rear of the antenna.

A German military policeman directing traffic signals the driver of an Sd.Kfz. 251 Ausf. C to stop for a streetcar in an Italian city: possibly Florence (Firenze), judging from the streets listed on the streetcar. The half-track has a name that appears to be "Bilichis" painted in Gothic letters below the visor. Below the name is stenciled data on nomenclature and weight for purposes of shipping the vehicle by railroad.

On a steppe in the Stalingrad area in late 1942, two Sd.Kfz. 251 Ausf. Cs of the 1st Cavalry Division scout for enemy positions. The soldier standing atop the nearer vehicle is surveying the terrain, using a scissors periscope. An abundance of gear is stowed on the two vehicles, including several Cossack sabers carried as trophies on the front of the closer half-track.

German vehicles with whitewash camouflage approach an engineer bridge in the USSR during the winter. The nearest one, an Sd.Kfz. 251 Ausf. C, has on its front plate the insignia of the 16th Panzer Division, a letter *Y* with a horizontal bar through it. The second vehicle appears to be a version of the Sd.Kfz. 251 with *schwere Wurfgerät* (heavy rocket launcher), but with the rockets and launcher racks not installed. In the right background is a *mittlerer Schützenpanzerwagen* (7.5 cm Kanone), also designated the Sd.Kfz. 251/9 Ausf. D.

General Hans-Jürgen von Arnim, commander of the Fifth Panzer Army in North Africa and later commander in chief of Army Group Africa, is in the front of an Sd.Kfz. 251 Ausf. C, next to the machine gun shield. On the front plate of the body is the symbol of the 21st Panzer Division, a capital letter *D* with a horizontal line through it.

The final model of the medium *Schützenpanzerwagen* was the Sd.Kfz. 251 Ausf. D. It entered operational service in 1943. Whereas the Ausf. C had three box-type stowage compartments on each fender, the Ausf. D had a faired structure from the fender up to the bottom of the upper side plates of the body, with three bottom-hinged access doors. Shown here is an Sd.Kfz. 251/1, the basic type configured for a panzergrenadier personnel carrier.

Another key feature of the Sd.Kfz. 251 Ausf. D was the simplified rear end, which eliminated the complex angles of the rear body and the bent doors in favor of a flat, backward-angled rear plate for the body and flat rear doors. In addition, the ventilation cowls on the sides of the hood were omitted; as a result, the side plates of the hood were flat.

The side of the body of the Sd.Kfz. 251 Ausf. D was redesigned at the rear to conform to the new, flat rear plate of the body. The bottom edge of the top plate of the side of the body extended several inches below where that plate was welded to the lower plate. A Notek blackout taillight is above the license plate. The crew step below the rear storage compartment was not a typical feature of the Ausf. D.

Another new feature of the Sd.Kfz. 251 Ausf. D was the elimination of the driver's and assistant driver's operable side visors, replaced with vision slits cut into the armor plate, with ballistic-glass blocks on the inner sides. Below the vision slit is a shipping stencil. Each stowage compartment door had a recess for a padlock and padlock hasp; each padlock was linked to the door with a retainer chain.

The front plate of the body of the Sd.Kfz. 251 Ausf. D was the same as that used on the Ausf. C and included a round plug for the opening for the crank for manually starting the engine. Another similarity with the Ausf. C was the lack of a front bumper. The muffler remained in the dip in the left fender.

This Sd.Kfz. 251 Ausf. D is equipped with two *Sternantennen*: star antennas with a vertical mast with upward-angled spoke-like elements at the top. These antennas commonly were associated with command vehicles. On the front plate of the body are the insignia of the 12th SS Panzer Division "Hitler-jugend" and the tactical symbol for a *Panzerfunken* (armored radio) unit.

Crewmen of an Sd.Kfz. 251 Ausf. D pose in their vehicle. This example has a variation of driver's and assistant driver's visors that had a flat frontal plate with a vision slit in it. Another variation of the visors seen on Sd.Kfz. 251 Ausf. Ds had a bulged frontal plate. Lined up on the roof of the cab are five Wehrmacht mess kits. *Thomas Anderson collection*

As seen on Sd.Kfz. 251 Ausf. D with license number WH-1542398, the fenders of this model were different than those on earlier models. Whereas earlier models had rolled fender edges, the fenders of the Ausf. D had edges that were bent at an obtuse angle to the adjoining part of the fender. The left fender on this vehicle has been crumpled. The vehicle has a sprayed-on squiggly camouflage pattern. A very faint tactical symbol for a half-track-towed howitzer battery is above the license plate. *Thomas Anderson collection*

An Sd.Kfz. 251 Ausf. D is positioned in a hayfield somewhere on the western front. Helmets with camouflage covers hang from the top of the body, and a rolled tarpaulin is lying on the cab roof. An MG 42 is on the rear mount. This vehicle had a Bosch headlight assembly on the left fender. *Thomas Anderson collection*

A GI contemplates a dead German soldier lying next to an abandoned Sd.Kfz. 251 Ausf. D, with spare track links stowed on the front plate of the vehicle and a generous supply of tree branches arranged on the vehicle for camouflage purposes. On the hood is a wooden frame with chicken wire attached to it. In the right background is an Sd.Kfz. 2 light half-track, better known as the *Kettenkraftrad*.

The crew of this Sd.Kfz. 251 Ausf. D went to great lengths to apply an elaborate array of tree branches on their vehicle. This so-called local camouflage hides the contours of most of the half-track while still allowing the gunner and the driver clear fields of vision toward the front. The forward machine gun mount has an armored shield.

Sd.Kfz. 251 Ausf. D half-tracks are lined up at the 12th SS Panzer Division "Hitlerjugend" training camp at Beverloo, Belgium, in early 1944 during an inspection by Field Marshal Gerd von Rundstedt. They are painted in faint camouflage patterns and have black vehicle numbers and black-and-white identification crosses on the sides.

An Sd.Kfz. 251 of the 5th SS Panzer Division "Wiking" tows a 7.5 cm Pak 40 antitank gun with dustcovers on the muzzle brake and the shield. On the left side of the rear of the vehicle's body is the insignia of the "Wiking" Division, while on the right side is the rectangular tactical symbol for an infantry unit.

Luftwaffe personnel, including several in *Fallschirmjäger* (paratrooper) smocks and helmets, gear up in an Sd.Kfz. 251 Ausf. D. A crude but effective camouflage scheme has been brushed on over the *Dunkelgelb* (dark yellow) base coat on the vehicle. The painter took care to cut in the inscription below the driver's side visor, although it is not sufficiently clear to determine if this was a railroad-loading stencil or a memorial inscription to a fallen crewman. *BA 580-1990-38A*

A dead German soldier lies on the road next to an abandoned Sd.Kfz. 251 Ausf. D with SS license plate. A shield for a front machine gun mount and, *to the far right*, part of a *Fliegerschwenkarm* machine gun mount are visible. On the road in the background is a tangle of shot-up vehicles, including a jeep. *Thomas Anderson collection*

The Sd.Kfz. 251 served in a multitude of roles, but surely one of the more unusual scenarios is depicted here, as an Ausf. D vehicle tows a string of six caravans across a railroad crossing. The half-track also is transporting a pole-shaped object with a white cover, possibly an artillery gun barrel, to the side of the machine gun shield.

At the scene of a combat action somewhere on the western front in early 1945, two knocked-out Sd.Kfz. 251s lie on a country lane. On the closer vehicle, the right front side apparently took a direct hit, rupturing the body, and the entire fender, storage compartments, and front wheel were torn off. The second vehicle is an Sd.Kfz. 251/9 Ausf. D, of the type armed with a 7.5 cm Kanone 51 on mount and shield above the body.

Germany's railroad system was a particular target of the Allies' strategic and tactical bombing campaigns, and this train loaded with vehicles at Saint-Clement, France, fell victim to an aerial attack around September 1944. On the flatcars are a variety of vehicle types, including at least four Sd.Kfz. 251 Ausf. Ds. Although the closest vehicle appears to be largely intact, the hood doors were blown off and the front tire was either burned off or blown off.

The Allies captured numbers of operable Sd.Kfz. 251s and put them to use, such as these two damaged but still-running examples employed by the 3rd Battalion, 11th Infantry Regiment, 5th Infantry Division, at Baden, Germany, during the advance to the Rhine River on March 7, 1945. To deter friendly fire, both half-tracks have crudely painted recognition stars on the hoods and the fronts; whereas the nearer vehicle has a star on the side of the body, the other one has a large "USA" on the side.

This restored Sd.Kfz. 251 Ausf. D is in the collection of Bob Graebe. Except for very early examples of the 251 Ausf. D, the fenders were much simpler than those of the C model, lacking the front turndowns of that model. With the built-in storage boxes of the D model, no rear fenders were required. The flared-out sections on the sides of the engine compartment were eliminated on the D model.

The rear of the armored body of the Sd.Kfz. 251 Ausf. D was flat and angled, with its top extending farther to the rear than the bottom. Consequently, the two doors on the rear of the body were flat too. The locking mechanism on the interior of the right door is in view. On the beam above the doors is a swivel mount for a machine gun.

More details of the rear doors are revealed. Above the license plate on the left mudguard is a Notek blackout convoy taillight. This taillight had a feature whereby it could be converted from a low-visibility light to a higher-visibility one.

Bench seats fabricated from wooden slats were frequently found in the Sd.Kfz. 251 Ausf. D, as a cost-cutting and production-speeding measure. These slats obviously are reproductions. The seat backs remained the upholstered, cushioned type.

Near the top of the right side of the fighting compartment, four flexible steel bows for supporting a canvas cover are stored in brackets. Behind the seat back are reproduction wooden rifle racks. *Rick Forys*

On the driver's compartment roof to the front of the MG 42 machine gun shield is a curved splash guard, to stop or deflect bullets or shrapnel from ricocheting into the fighting compartment. A radio antenna is on the far side of the machine gun. Also in view are the driver's visor and the vision slit cut into the side of the armored body.

The 7.92 mm MG 42, its mount, and its armor shield are installed atop the driver's compartment roof. The German term for this style of machine gun mount was *Schwenkarm* (swivel arm). *Rick Forys*

The right side of the driver's compartment is shown. On the ceiling is a crash pad, to protect the occupant of the right seat from head injuries from the jouncing of the vehicle. A similar pad was provided for the driver. Above the MP 40 9 mm submachine gun is a bracket for inserting a glass vision block behind the vision slit. On the front of the compartment is the right front visor, showing the operating lever. *Rick Forys*

The driver's station is viewed from behind the right seat, showing the tilted steering wheel; instrument panel; accelerator, clutch, and brake pedals; and control levers. Those levers are, *left to right*, reduction gear shifter, hand brake, and transmission gearshift. *Rick Forys*

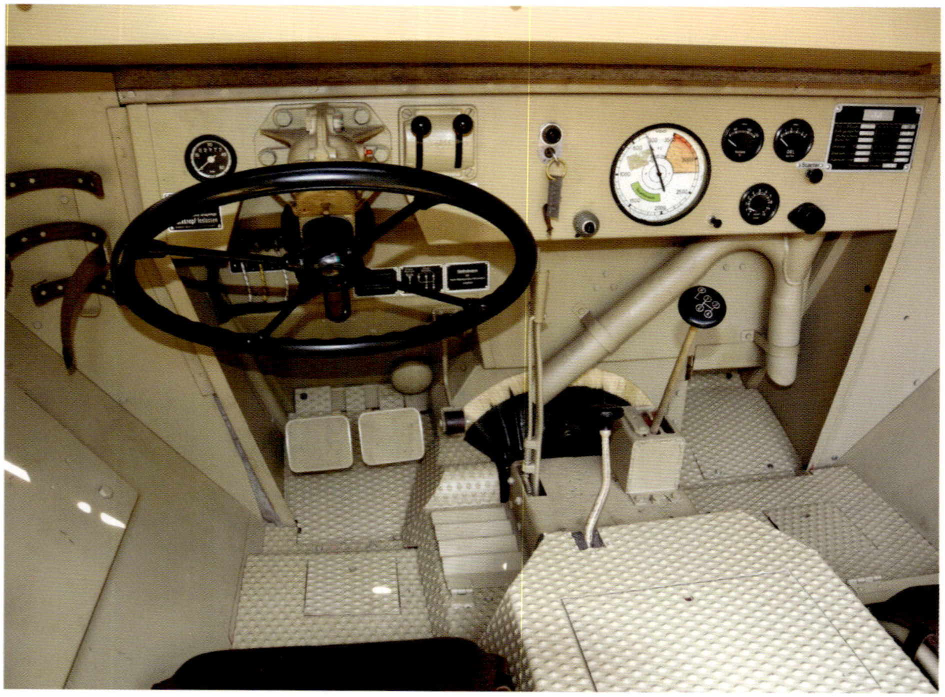

Further details of the instrument panel, steering wheel, and controls are displayed. The large white gauge is the tachometer. Toward the left, on the right side of the data plate, is the starter button. Impressed on the knob of the transmission gear shifter is a diagram of the shifting pattern, which included one reverse and four forward gears. *Rick Forys*

The Sd.Kfz. 251 Ausf. D in the collection of Bob Graebe was restored with a two-color camouflage scheme of dark yellow and green. Reproduction markings include an SS license plate, the divisional sign of "Liebstandarte SS Adolf Hitler," and the tactical sign for a heavy reconnaissance company. *Rick Forys*

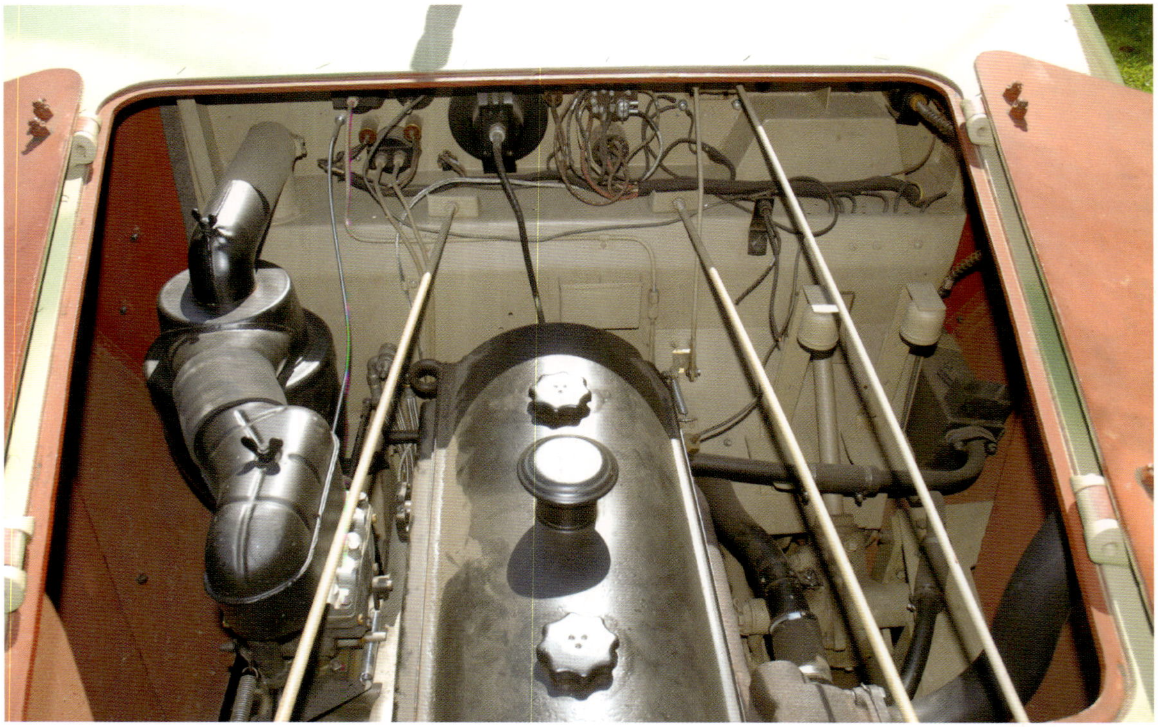

Inside the front of the Sd.Kfz. 251 Ausf. D is the Maybach HL 42 TUKRRM engine, a six-cylinder, in-line, water-cooled design with a displacement of 4.17 liters and a rating of 100 horsepower at 2,800 rpm. To the left are the air cleaner and the carburetor, while to the right is the engine exhaust.

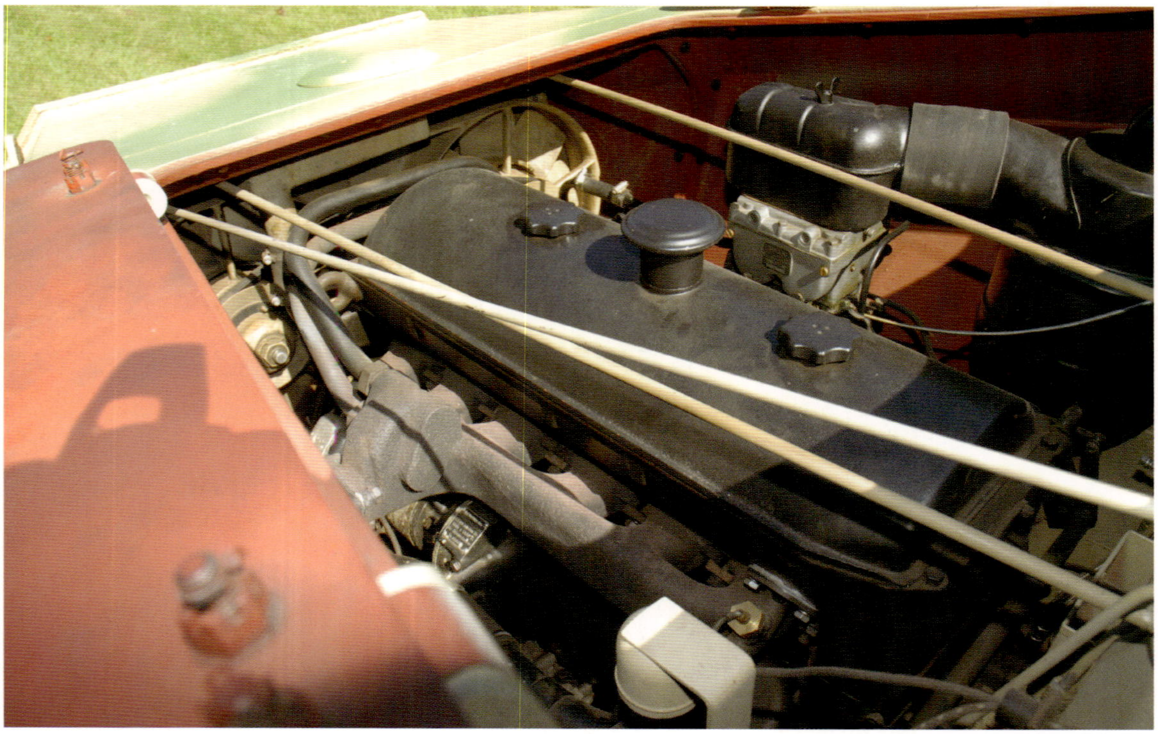

The engine compartment is viewed from the left side facing forward, with the air cleaner and carburetor in the background, the valve cover at the center, the exhaust manifold on the left, and the two cooling fans in the front of the compartment.

CHAPTER 2

The Many Variants of the Sd.Kfz. 251

As will be seen, the Sd.Kfz. 251 was produced in many variations (or *Ausführung*), but notably not all models were produced in every (Ausf. A, B, C, and D) body style. The basic vehicle, or armored personnel carrier, was designated Sd.Kfz. 251/1. After World War II, the design was slightly modified to become the diesel-powered, fully enclosed OT-810 used by Czechoslovakia.

Rocket Launchers

Beginning in 1941, a popular modification to the Sd.Kfz. 251 was the installation of launchers for 28 or 32 cm rockets, known as *schwere Wurfgerät*. The rocket system, the *Wurfrahmen* 40, or launch frame (19)40, consisted of a framework with three adjustable baseplates installed along each side of the half-track body. Traverse was controlled by positioning of the vehicle through using aiming rods attached to the front of the vehicle. Elevation was adjustable on each launcher. Three calibers of rockets were available: a 300 mm high explosive as well as 280 mm and 320 mm incendiary rockets. The rockets' shipping crates doubled as the launch housing and were hung on the baseplates alongside the vehicle. Range, depending upon rocket, varied from 975 to 4,550 meters.

The exhaust from the rockets required that the crew leave the vehicle prior to firing the rockets. These launchers are known to have been mounted on infantry carriers and engineer half-tracks, and the vehicle crew consisted of one driver, two gunners, and a vehicle commander.

Sd.Kfz. 251/2

In September 1940, development of a mortar carrier based on the Sd.Kfz. 251 was begun. A vehicle with the *schwerer Granatwerfer* 34 8.0 cm mortar was tested in the spring of 1941 and found to be a success. Dubbed the Sd.Kfz. 251/2, the vehicle was laid out so that the mortar could fire from inside a stationary half-track. The flight path of the shell required the deletion of the forward machine gun.

A conventional mortar baseplate was carried on the outside of the half-track, allowing the mortar to also be used as a dismounted weapon. While most of the mortar carriers were built in earlier bodies, some were created with the Ausf. D body. Provision was made in the 8.64-ton half-track to stow sixty-six rounds of mortar ammunition, as well as to transport the crew of eight.

Sd.Kfz. 251/3 *Funkpanzerwagen*

The 251/3 was listed in the August 13, 1942, D-660/7 loading manual as an artillery-towing vehicle. By February 10, 1943, the Sd.Kfz. 251/3 had begun to be listed as a *Funkpanzerwagen*, or communications vehicle. The bulk of the Sd.Kfz. 251/3 production was based on the Ausf. D body, although some were built with the Ausf. C body.

By August 8, 1944, seven subvariants of the Sd.Kfz. 251/3 were classified as follows:

- Sd.Kfz. 251/3 I, equipped with FuG. 8, FuG. 4, and Fu.Spr.Ger.f
- Sd.Kfz. 251/3 IIa, equipped with FuG. 8, FuG. 5, FuG. 4, and Fu.Spr.Ger.f
- Sd.Kfz. 251/3 IIb, equipped with FuG. 12, FuG. 5, FuG. 4, and Fu.Spr.Ger.f
- Sd.Kfz. 251/3 III, equipped with FuG. 7, FuG. 1, and Fu.Spr.Ger.f
- Sd.Kfz. 251/3 IIIa, equipped with FuG. 12, FuG. 1, and Fu.Spr.Ger.f
- Sd.Kfz. 251/3 IV, equipped with FuG. 11 and FuG. 12
- Sd.Kfz. 251/3 V, equipped with FuG. 11

The Sd.Kfz. 251/3 IV replaced the Sd.Kfz. 251/6 and was designated m.Funk-Pz.Wg. (Kdo.Wg), or medium radio command vehicle.

Each version of the 8.5-ton half-track was crewed by seven men. They were initially armed with two 7.92 mm MG 34s, which by January 27, 1944, had given way to an equal number of 7.92 mm MG 42s (depending on year) with 2,010 rounds of ammunition.

Sd.Kfz. 251/4 *mittlerer SchützenPanzerwagen (IG)*

These vehicles, constructed in the form of the Ausf. A, Ausf. B, and Ausf. C, had the forward portion of their rear seating replaced with ammo racks. These racks held 120 rounds of 7.5 cm (75 mm) ammunition for the 7.5 cm *leichtes Infanteriegeschütz* 18 (le.I.G.18), or light infantry support gun—essentially a small field howitzer.

In time, the designation was also applied to vehicles used as a prime mover for that same weapon, as well as the 15 cm s.I.G., 5 cm PaK, and 7.5 cm PaK. January 1944 documents indicate that the 251/4 was to be dropped from future production, an action that had been taken by November of that year.

Beginning in 1941 the Sd.Kfz. 251 was used as a platform for the *schwere Wurfgerät* 40 (heavy rocket launcher type 40). Six of the launcher racks and rockets were mounted on the *schwere Wurfrahmen 40* (heavy launching-frame type 40), three per side. Either a 28 cm high-explosive rocket or a 32 cm rocket with a napalm-like mix of oil and high explosive could be used. The ignition system for the rockets was electrical. The elevation of the launchers was adjustable, but to adjust the azimuth, the entire vehicle was aimed at the target. To assist in this, aiming vanes were used; one is mounted on the front of the hood. *Bundesarchiv*

Sd.Kfz. 251/5 *mittlerer SchützenPanzerwagen (Pi)*

The Sd.Kfz. 251 began to be supplied to Pioniere, or Engineer, troops in 1939. Initially, the vehicles were standard Sd.Kfz. 251/1, but the troops installed racks inside the half-tracks for the engineer equipment. This equipment was stowed in the rear half of the body opposite the driver. On November 16, 1940, this type vehicle was classified Sd.Kfz. 251/5 *mittlerer SchützenPanzerwagen* (Pi).

The crew and armament of the Engineer half-track varied over the years, from eight to nine men, and sometimes with one and other times two machine guns. In 1943 the Sd.Kfz. 251/7 was introduced as a replacement for the Sd.Kfz. 251/5, and in January of the next year, plans were made to cease production of the /5, with the Sd.Kfz. 251/7 replacing it. This action had been taken by November 1944.

Sd.Kfz. 251/6 *mittlerer KommandoPanzerwagen*

This vehicle is often confused with the similar Sd.Kfz. 251/3. However, the 8.5-ton Sd.Kfz. 251/6 was equipped with one each of the 80-watt FuG 12 and 15-watt FuG 19 radio sets. A crew of eight served the vehicle.

Some of these half-tracks were equipped with the famous Enigma cryptographic device.

Sd.Kfz. 251/6s assigned to Luftwaffe units for use by "Flivos" (*Fliegerverbindugsoffizier*, or air force liaison officer—essentially a forward air controller) were sometimes equipped with 10-meter pole-type antennas. On some Ausf. A and Ausf. B-bodied versions, a map table was field-installed over the driver's compartment.

Sd.Kfz. 251/7 *mittlerer PionierePanzerwagen*

An improvement on the earlier Sd.Kfz. 251/5, the 251/7 was produced using Ausf. C- and Ausf. D-hulled vehicles. Like the earlier model, extensive engineer equipment was stowed in special compartments internally, but in the case of the Sd.Kfz. 251/7, two portable bridge sections of 8-ton capacity were carried on racks, one on each side of the body.

Introduced in late 1940, the *mittlerer Pioniere Panzerwagen* remained in production by Weserhütte through March 1945. Initially armed with the MG 34, the eight-man crews of later models defended themselves with two MG 42s. Every other vehicle, numbers 2, 4, and 6 in a platoon, was also equipped with a Pz.B.39 antitank rifle. By November 1944, an MP 40 machine pistol replaced one of the MG 42 machine guns. Some of the earlier vehicles had no radio, but beginning in 1942, the engineer half-tracks were equipped with the Fu.Spr.Ger.f radio set mounted in front of the codriver. Beginning in 1943, some 251/7s were fitted with the Fu. 5 radio set. These vehicles were designated Sd. Kfz. 251/7 II.

Sd.Kfz. 251/8 *mittlerer KrankenPanzerwagen*

The Sd.Kfz. 251/8 was a half-track especially outfitted for use as an armored battlefield ambulance. As such, it had no mounted weapons. Other differences included the installation of a large water container mounted on the floor above the transmission, and, most significantly, replacing the normal seating and equipment stowage with special seats and litter racks. Occasionally, conventional Sd.Kfz. 251s were pressed into service as ambulances, but these can be distinguished from the special vehicles by the presence of weapons mounts (but not the weapons themselves). A two-man crew served the 7.47-ton vehicle.

251/9 m Schütz Pz Wg (7.5 cm K) *Kanonenwagen* "Stummel"

The increasing need for a fire support vehicle based on the medium half-track fortunately coincided with the rearming of the *Sturmgeschütz* with long guns. The design, commissioned from Büssing-NAG in March 1942, involved mounting the 7.5 cm K51 L/24 short guns removed from the assault guns as they were rearmed. These were installed in the Sd.Kfz. 251 by using a mounting based on that developed for the *Sturmgeschütz*. The short barrel of the Sd.Kfz. 251/9's cannon earned it the nickname "Stummel," or stump.

The nature of the installation required radical changes to the half-track. As well as deletion of the forward machine gun mount, a large portion of the frontal armor was cut away in the area normally used by the codriver. This change was made so that the new gun could be mounted partially inset into the profile of the vehicle, minimizing its height. The left rear seat was removed, making room for stowage for fifty-two rounds of main gun ammunition. The radio was relocated to the left sidewall in order to accommodate the cannon and its mount. Installation of the KwK pushed the vehicle's weight up to 8.53 tons, and its height to 2.07 meters.

Production of the first order for the new Sd.Kfz. 251/9 began in June 1942, following the successful test of two trial vehicles earlier that month on the Russian front. Production of the Sd. Kfz. 251/9 with 7.5 cm K51 L/24 had reached 630 units by December 1943, when the design was changed.

Beginning in December 1943, the Sd.Kfz. 251/9 began to be produced using the 7.5 cm K51 (sf) and a simplified mounting. This mounting did not require the major cutting away of the frontal armor as was necessitated for the earlier mount. Instead, the weapon was mounted on top of the superstructure above the driver and codriver.

A new armored shield was created to protect the crew in this new, more exposed, position. Beyond expediting production, the new mounting also had the advantage of 20-degree traverse to either side, as opposed to the 12-degree right and 10-degree left traverse of the 7.5 cm Kanone L/24. A flexible MG 42 was mounted on the right side of the gun shield. From January through November

With the rockets and launchers not installed on this *schwere Wurfgerät* on an Sd.Kfz. 251 Ausf. B., a clear view is available of the tubular frames with vertical plates that support the launcher mounts. The mounts comprise smaller plates that pivot on the larger plates to the desired elevation. On each of the smaller plates are two pivoting arms that support the launcher and rocket; those arms are seen here in the raised position for travel.

A *schwere Wurfgerät* on an Sd.Kfz. 251 is observed from above the hood, without rockets and launchers installed. The front and the rear of the frame were secured by tubular cross members, and in between those members the frame was attached to the top edge of the body.

1944, 1,090 of the improved vehicle with 7.5 cm K51 (sf) cannon had been produced.

At Hitler's orders, the Sd.Kfz. 251/9 was superseded in production by the Sd.Kfz. 251/22, with Wumag producing the final two Stummels in December 1944.

Sd.Kfz. 251/10 *mittlerer Schützen-Panzerwagen* (3.7 cm PaK)

Used as a platoon leader's vehicle, it was intended that this 3.7 cm antitank, gun-armed variant of the Sd.Kfz. 251 would give each platoon a little heavier punch, and an integral defense against tanks and other hard targets. Rheinmetall delivered a trial vehicle in May 1941, and production began soon after, with eighty units being delivered in July–August 1941. Production continued until at least October 1943, but by January of the following year, it had been decided to drop the type from production. Organizationally, the Sd.Kfz. 251/10 was replaced by the Sd.Kfz. 251/17.

In the Sd.Kfz. 251/10, a 3.7 cm PaK 36 was mounted above the driver and codriver in lieu of the machine gun normally found in that location. Various gun shields were used, ranging for the standard PaK 36 shield to low-profile shields to a shield on one side only. Some even had no shield at all.

The 8.01-ton half-track transported its crew of five or six men, as well as 168 rounds of ammunition. A machine gun, either MG 34 or MG 42, was mounted on the rear of the vehicle. It was provided with 1,100 rounds of ammunition.

Sd.Kfz. 251/11 *mittlerer FernsprechPanzerwagen*

This vehicle, initially produced in the Ausf. C body, was built for use in laying telephone cable, as well as housing telephone exchange equipment. Delivery of the vehicles began in August of 1942, and production was scheduled to continue until February 1945.

Two versions of a telephone-cable-laying half-track were built.

One type was equipped with the leichter Feldkabelträger 6 (light field cable carrier), the other with the mittlerer Feldkabelträger 10.

In either case, a cabinet with cable reels and telephone equipment replaced the two right-hand bench seats. A third cable reel was mounted on the left fender. The crew of five used long staffs to hang the cable in trees and bushes.

The 8.5-ton vehicle retained the normal two-machine gun armament found on most Sd.Kfz. 251s.

Sd.Kfz. 251/12 *mittlerer Messtrupp and Gerätpanzerwagen*, Sd.Kfz. 251/13 *mittlerer Schallaufnahmepanzerwagen*, Sd.Kfz. 251/14 *mittlerer Schallauswertepanzerwagen*, Sd.Kfz. 251/15 *mittlerer Lichtauswertepanzerwagen*

These half-tracks, which were to be equipped with various sound- and flash-ranging equipment for panzer divisions, are listed in the July 1943 operators manual.

However, no record, document, or photograph has yet surfaced to provide evidence that any of these were actually produced.

Sd.Kfz. 251/16 *mittlerer Flammpanzerwagen*

The Sd.Kfz. 251 was first used to mount flamethrowers, beginning with the Ausf. C chassis, in January 1943. When the Ausf. C body was dropped in favor of the Ausf. D, production of the flamethrower-equipped version continued. Ultimately, over 350 were produced.

As initially configured, the flame-throwing half-track, which was designated Sd.Kfz. 251/16, was equipped with two mounted 14 mm flame projectors and a portable, but tethered, 7 mm projector.

The 14 mm projectors were mounted on either side of the hull in a staggered manner. Their mountings allowed them to be traversed 160 degrees. Two flame oil containers, one mounted inside each rear sidewall, held a combined 700 liters of fuel. This allowed approximately eighty one-second bursts to be fired. A Koebe pumping system, powered by a separate Auto Union 28-horsepower engine, supplied the fuel to the projectors. The

Rockets and their frame-type launchers are installed on a *schwere Wurfgerät* on an Sd.Kfz. 251 Ausf. B. The *schwere Wurfgerät* 40 launcher frames were fabricated of wood. The rockets were spin-stabilized. The 28 cm high-explosive type weighed 181 pounds and had a maximum range of 1.2 miles, while the 32 cm rockets weighed 174 pounds and had a maximum range of 1.37 miles.

range of the flamethrowers was 50 to 60 meters. Ignition of the 14 mm flame projectors was electric, with cartridge ignition for the portable projector.

In May 1944 the Sd.Kfz. 251/16 was revamped. The side-mounted flame projectors were redesigned to use cartridge rather than electric ignition. At the same time, the handheld unit was deleted as being impractical, cumbersome, and little used.

In addition to the flame projectors, the four-man crew of the 8.62-ton half-track had the forward MG 34 at their disposal. The vehicle commander doubled as radio operator, while each mounted projector had its own operator, and of course the fourth man drove the vehicle.

Sd.Kfz. 251/17 *mittlerer SchützenPanzerwagen* (2 cm)

Although some medium half-tracks had been previously modified to act as antiaircraft vehicles, the Sd.Kfz. 251/17 was the first officially manufactured one. Production of this variant was planned to begin in November 1944, with projections calling for 390 to be built by Schichau and 822 by Weserhütte by December of the following year.

However, a September 1, 1944, inventory list by the Panzerkraftwagen und Zugkraftwagenabteilung Amtsgruppe fur Industrielle Rustang—Waffen und Gerät (Wa J Rue), or, more simply put, Tanks and Tractors Branch, Group for Weapons and Equipment Manufacture, already showed fifty-four Sd.Kfz. 251/17s on hand.

A 2 cm FlaK 38 was pedestal mounted in the rear of the vehicle.

The gunner's seat was attached to the mount and moved along with the gun as it was traversed and elevated via handwheels. Ammunition was fed to the weapon via twenty-round magazines. A crew of four served the vehicle, which was not a total success due in part to the cramped confines of the 251's hull. The rear MG 42 was retained for self-defense.

Sd.Kfz. 251/18 *mittlerer Beobachtungspanzerwagen*

These vehicles were intended to replace the smaller Sd.Kfz. 250/5 light observation half-tracks. Four variants of the new *mittlerer Beobachtungspanzerwagen* were introduced in August 1944; the versions differed in radio equipment. The Sd.Kfz. 251/18 I was equipped with Fu 8, Fu 4, and Fu.Spr.Ger.f radio sets. The Sd.Kfz. 251/18 Ia was the same, but for the deletion of the Fu.Spr.Ger.f set.

The Sd.Kfz. 251/18 II mounted the Fu 5 and Fu 8 sets, while the IIa added a Fu 4 to the II's equipment ensemble.

Schichau was tasked with assembling the 8.5-ton vehicles, which carried a varying number of crewmen depending on model and task.

Sd.Kfz. 251/19 *mittlerer Fernsprechbetriebspanzerwagen*

This medium half-track was equipped as a mobile telephone exchange. It was used by signals units to provide rapid ground communications among units of advancing armies. These vehicles were built in both the Ausf. C and Ausf. D hulls.

The rockets and their launchers, which also doubled as shipping containers, were transported inside the Sd.Kfz. 251 and were installed on the launching mounts once the vehicle was emplaced for firing. The middle crosspiece on each of these launching frames is marked "MB 50." There was just enough room to the fronts of the rockets for a crewman to stand up.

A man—it is unclear if he is an Allied soldier, a POW, or a civilian—removes a rocket from the interior of an abandoned Sd.Kfz. 251 with *schwere Wurfgerät*. Signs that read "BOOBY TRAPS" are in the foreground. To the left and right side of the photo are storage bins of sheet metal fabrication with lids open that are fastened with U-brackets to the tubular frame for the rocket launchers.

The interior of the vehicle is viewed toward the rear, showing three crewmen seated in very cramped conditions to the rear of the stored rockets. The crew consisted of the commander, the driver, and two gunners. The rockets were transported in the vehicle two tiers high.

German soldiers wrestle a rocket and launcher rack onto the mount on the side of an Sd.Kfz. 251 Ausf. C. Once the rocket was emplaced on the mount, the cross-slat at the front of the launcher frame was removed and the fuse was inserted in the nose of the rocket. *BA 216-0417-03*

A crewman clamps a rocket launcher onto the center mount on the right side of an Sd.Kfz. 251. To the right, details of the rear mount are visible. The support arms are lowered; below them is an elevation scale, affixed to the stationary vertical plate, and an elevation indicator, attached to the swiveling mount. To set the elevation for the rockets, the swiveling plate was pushed into the desired angle and then clamped. *BA 216-0417-06*

Sd.Kfz. 251/20 *mittlerer SchützenPanzerwagen* (Uhu)

Germany was very interested in developing night-fighting capabilities for their army and had begun work toward this in the late 1930s. By 1944, a night-fighting system for the Panther had been developed. However, one of the shortcomings of this system was the limited range of visibility provided by the 20 cm infrared searchlight mounted on the tank, which limited the vision of the crew to only 100–200 meters. The obvious solution was a larger, more powerful infrared searchlight. With space on and in the tank being limited, the solution was to mount a larger searchlight on the Sd.Kfz. 251 Ausf. D half-track.

Classified as the Sd.Kfz. 251/20, one of the 9.3-ton vehicles was to be assigned to each six IR-equipped Panthers. The Sd. Kfz. 251/20 was equipped with a 60 cm IR searchlight in the rear, attached to a rotating and pivoting mount, and a smaller 20 cm IR searchlight attached to the cowl just forward of the windshield. Also installed on the vehicle were BG 1251 and FG 1252 infrared scopes, a MG 42, and radio equipment. Wumag was to assemble the half-tracks with IR equipment, and they began doing just that in January 1945. The combination infrared searchlight and scope was code-named “Uhu”—eagle-owl.

The same crewmen seen in the preceding photo now are maneuvering a rocket launcher onto the front right mount on the Sd.Kfz. 251. Two other launchers already are mounted. Note the MG 34 mounted above the cab. *BA 216-0417-04*

Documentation has surfaced to verify only one use of this equipment, which occurred on March 26, 1945. This action was by 1.Kompanie / Panzer-Abteilung 101 of the Führer-Grenadier Division. The unit had three Sd.Kfz. 251/20 Uhus to be used with ten Panther tanks with FG 1250 infrared sights.

Reportedly, some of the Uhu-equipped 251s had their generators and large searchlights removed, providing a partial IR-equipped armored personnel carrier for supporting infantry. These vehicles were dubbed "Falke," or Falcon. The remaining smaller searchlight, walkways, etc. remained in situ on these vehicles, and they continued to have Sd.Kfz. 251/20 stenciled on their shipping data.

Sd.Kfz. 251/21 *mittlerer Schützen-Panzerwagen* (MG 151S)

As Allied air supremacy continued to increase, so did the need for Germany to develop adequate mobile antiaircraft protection both for armored and infantry units. One of the vehicles built to fill this role was the Sd.Kfz. 251/21.

Drawn up in July 1944, this medium half-track had mounted in its rear a triple 1.5 cm machine gun mount known as the Drilling. The Mauser MG 151 machine guns had originally been developed for use on aircraft but had since been supplanted as aerial weapons.

The weapons were aimed manually, using either optical or, later, ring-and-bead sights. The standard Sd.Kfz. 251 rear bench seats were replaced by a single-person seat on the right and two single-person seats on the left. Ammunition bins, one large and two small, were located inside the rear of the vehicle. The guns were fed ammo from chests containing 250 rounds each in the case of the outer weapons, and 400 rounds in the center chest. Spent shell casings were collected in the pedestal. The rear MG 42 continued to be mounted for self-defense.

Production of the Sd.Kfz. 251/21 began in August 1944 and continued as described above into December 1944. At that time, more powerful 2 cm MG 151 heavy machine guns began to be mounted in lieu of the 1.5 cm guns. It is known that the vehicles remained in production into February 1945; however, the records for later periods have been lost.

Sd.Kfz. 251/22 *mittlerer Schützenpanzerwagen* (7.5 cm PaK)

In late 1944, Hitler decreed that all suitable motor vehicle chassis were to be adapted to serve as *Panzerjäger*. Thus, using a mounting similar to that used on the Sd.Kfz. 234/4 armored car, the 7.5 cm PaK 40 was shoehorned into a medium half-track.

Two heavy steel beams were installed in the rear hull, sloping from front to rear. These served as the foundation for the gun mount, which was essentially the same as used by the towed PaK 40, save for the omission of the carriage. The gun shield had

Three soldiers carry a rocket and its launcher for the *schwere Wurfgerät.* The base of the rocket is visible inside the launcher frame, with its small, round rocket ports arrayed around the perimeter of the base. *BA 216-0417-05*

"Tilsit" is the nickname painted on the ventilator cowl of this Sd.Kfz. 251 Ausf. C with *schwere Wurfgerät.* The rockets are the 32 cm type, and the fuses are not yet inserted in their noses. A sprayed-on camouflage paint pattern is visible on the body of the vehicle and the shield for the MG 34. *Patton Museum*

Two rockets and their launching racks are installed in this photo. The launching racks were of fairly crude construction. Inside the racks, strips of wood secured in place by L-shaped metal brackets served to hold the rocket motors to the rears of the projectiles.

to be modified, with part of the lower corners cut away to permit traverse, as did the half-track.

A portion of the driver's compartment roof was removed to allow clearance for the gun's recoil cylinder. Naturally, the interior stowage was heavily modified, with the forward rear seats and rifle racks being removed, as well as the commander's seat. A travel lock was added to the outside of the vehicle, and ammunition lockers to the interior.

A four-man crew served the vehicle, and they had a single MG 42 with which to defend the vehicle from infantry attack. Production of the Sd.Kfz. 251/22 began in December 1944. Production was concentrated at Wumag, which fell to the Soviets in February 1945. Beyond this, there were efforts to field-modify vehicles into the 251/22 configuration. This modification consisted chiefly of converting Sd.Kfz. 251/9 to Sd.Kfz. 251/22 configuration.

2 cm FlaK 38 *auf Schützenpanzerwagen* Sd.Kfz. 251

A small group of perhaps one dozen Sd.Kfz. 251 Ausf. C were modified for the Luftwaffe to act as antiaircraft vehicles (ten were gun vehicles; the other two were command vehicles). These half-tracks had a complete 2 cm FlaK 38 mount installed in the rear. In order to provide clearance for the mount, the hull side plates were extended, making the vehicle rather resemble the Sd. Kfz. 250 alte.

However, in addition to the extension, much of the hull sides were also hinged, allowing them to fold down. This not only provided for the gun to traverse 360 degrees but also allowed the weapon to be depressed enough to engage ground targets. There was also sufficient room for the crew to serve the weapon. These vehicles were used in field trials, but due to the complexity and expense of the conversion, they were not adopted as standard. These vehicles should not be confused with the later Sd.Kfz. 251/17, which did not have folding side armor.

The *schwere Wurfgerät* 40 was installed on all four submodels of the Sd.Kfz. 251, such as this Ausf. A or B vehicle. The clamp handles for securing the launchers at the desired elevations are visible above the elevation scales. Sources vary on the range of elevation of the *schwere Wurfgerät* 40, but authorities Thomas Jentz and Hilary Doyle recorded that it was from 16 to 45 degrees. *Patton Museum*

The rockets were fired at brief intervals, not in one instantaneous salvo, and all six rockets could be launched within ten seconds. The rockets were not particularly accurate, but their effect could be shocking in an area bombardment. This potential for a sudden and impressive bombardment led to the nickname often bestowed on this vehicle: *Stuka-zu-Fuß* (Stuka on foot). *Patton Museum*

At times the Sd.Kfz. 251 with *schwere Wurfgerät* was expected to perform the duties of a personnel carrier, as in this example that is filled with troops, with the machine gunner evidently on guard against enemy threats across the railroad embankment. A second MG 34 is on the rear antiaircraft swivel-arm mount.

An example of a camouflage-painted Sd.Kfz. Ausf. D with *schwere Wurfgerät* without rockets installed is shown. The pivoting plates and folding arms that cradled the rocket launchers are locked at maximum elevation. On the forward gun mount is an MG 42 machine gun. Since the frame of the rocket launchers interfered with the operation of the storage compartment doors on the side of the body, crews tended to stow items of equipment in the spaces between the body and the fixed vertical plates of the launchers. *Patton Museum*

Sd.Kfz. 251/2

After the Sd.Kfz. 251/1, the basic personnel carrier version, the first numbered variant of the vehicle was the Sd.Kfz. 251/2, an armored carrier for the 8 cm Gr.W.34 mortar. In this photo of an Sd.Kfz. 251/2, the muzzle of the forward-pointing mortar is just visible above the top of the personnel compartment. The weapon could be fired from the vehicle, or it could be set up on a base-plate outside the vehicle for firing.

The interior of an Sd.Kfz. 251/2 is viewed from the right side. The mortar base rests in a socket on the floor between the crew seats, and the upper part of the mortar tube is supported by a bipod. Rifles are stored behind the front seat back. To the right is the cab, and to the left are the rear doors, with a fire extinguisher stored on the right door.

Two crewmen are operating the 8 cm Gr.W.34 mortar in an Sd.Kfz. 251/2. The mortarman to the right is viewing through the panoramic sight. The hand on the opposite side of the mortar from the sight is operating the traversing knob. The mortar had a maximum range of 2,624 yards. *BA 732-0111-16A*

Field Marshal Gerd von Rundstedt and his staff walk past a row of Sd.Kfz. 251/2 mortar carriers during his inspection of the 12th SS Panzer Division "Hitlerjugend" at the Beverloo training camp in Belgium in early 1944. These vehicles lacked front machine gun mounts, which would have impeded the forward fire of the mortars. At least the nearest two vehicles were radio equipped, while the third vehicle is an Sd.Kfz. 251/9. *BA 297-1740-06A*

Sd.Kfz. 251/3

The first iteration of the Sd.Kfz. 251/3 was an artillery prime mover, but by early February 1943 that designation had been bestowed on a new submodel, the *mittlerer Funkpanzerwagen* (medium radio carrier). A pilot medium radio carrier, based on Sd.Kfz. 251 Ausf. C with license number WH-1451971, is seen here. Note the *Sternantenne* (star antenna) on the left rear corner of the body; the upward-angled spokes of the "star" part of the antenna are visible above the roof of the building.

An Sd.Kfz. 251/3 assigned to an infantry company sits outside a town on the eastern front. On the rear of the vehicle is an insignia in the shape of an inverted *Y*. This would have been for the 1st Panzer Division, unless there was a small vertical bar to the right of the symbol that has been obscured, in which case it would be for the 2nd Panzer Division. A mast for a star antenna is on the left rear corner of the body; the antenna mount was quite exposed in this location and later would receive an armored shield.

This photograph and the following two images document an inspection of the 12th SS Panzer Division "Hitlerjugend" by Field Marshal Gerd von Rundstedt at the Beverloo training camp in Belgium in early 1944. Here, Rundstedt stands in the front passenger's door of an Sd.Kfz. 8 half-track. To the left is an Sd.Kfz. 251/3 Ausf. D *mittlerer Funkpanzerwagen* numbered 001. The base for the star antenna now has an armored shield.

Field Marshal von Rundstedt, *right*, and his staff pass by the Sd.Kfz. 251/3 Ausf. D numbered 001 during the review at Beverloo. A modification seen on top of the cab is the spotlight. A scissors periscope is to the rear of the spotlight. A rod antenna is mounted on the side of the personnel compartment.

Von Rundstedt and entourage are viewed from the hood of the Sd.Kfz. 251/3 Ausf. D seen in the preceding photos. There were several marks of the Sd.Kfz. 251/3, on the basis of the purpose of the vehicle and the equipment carried. The spotlight (*lower left*) and the scissors periscope are seen from another angle, as is the shield for the stern antenna mount.

Another Sd.Kfz. 251/3 is viewed from the rear, offering another look at the armored shield for the star antenna base. One of the elements of the star is badly bent. Concerning the number on the rear of the vehicle, the letter *I* stands for 1st Battalion, and 02 means that this was the vehicle of the assistant commander, or executive officer, of the battalion.

Several different types of antenna were in use on Sd.Kfz. 251/3s, depending on the radio sets carried. Two are visible on this vehicle: a 2-meter star antenna on the left rear of the body, and a 9-meter winch mast, a telescoping-mast design shown in the lowered position. Bows to support a tarpaulin cover for the personnel compartment are installed.

Sd.Kfz. 251/6

The Sd.Kfz. 251/6 *mittlerer Kommandopanzerwagen* was a medium armored command half-track. Assigned to upper-echelon commanders, they were equipped with Fu. 12 and Fu. 19 radio sets, decoding and encoding equipment, and, from 1942 on, a *Funksprechgerät a* radio. The Sd.Kfz. 251/6 featured a prominent frame antenna above the vehicle, as seen on this Ausf. A example.

The crew of this Sd.Kfz. 251/6 Ausf. A has lashed a makeshift awning on the frame antenna, using what appear to be shelter halves, one of which is camouflaged. Both machine gun mounts had shields. To the right rear of the vehicle is a winch mast, a telescoping, winch-operated mast with a star or umbrella antenna on top. *BA 187-0208-27*

A crewman climbs into an Sd.Kfz. 251/6 Ausf. A. This vehicle had a step below the left door, possibly a field modification. Arrayed along the right side of the interior are radio sets on racks. The operators sat in seats along the left side of the compartment. *Patton Museum*

General Heinz Guderian (*far right*), commander of XIX Panzer Corps and one of the principal architects of Germany's armored forces, and members of his staff are in an Sd.Kfz. 251/6 Ausf. A command vehicle during the 1940 invasion of France. The view is from the right side of the vehicle. Note the wire lead from the frame antenna to the left and the shroud to protect the wire where it crosses over the top edge of the armor. *Patton Museum*

Another photo of Guderian in an Sd.Kfz. 251/6 Ausf. A in France in 1940 shows the rear of the personnel compartment. In the left foreground is a Wehrmacht Enigma I cypher machine. The Enigma I used three rotors at a time (visible just to the left of the keyboard) out of five issued with the machine. The German navy used a six-rotor Enigma, and an eight-rotor model was also produced for high-level communications. *BA 769-0229-12A*

Another photo of General Guderian in an Sd.Kfz. 251/6 Ausf. A reveals that a letter *G* also was painted on the left fender. Next to that letter is the tactical symbol for a communications company. The forward MG 34 is on an antiaircraft swiveling-arm mount.

A final photo of Guderian in an Sd.Kfz. 251/6 Ausf. A in France in 1940 shows a tarpaulin pulled back over the rear of the personnel compartment. Stored on the side of the body are a crowbar and a crank for manually starting the engine. On the left rear door is the letter *G* with two dots to the right of it: The G was a marking particular to Panzergruppe Guderian.

An Sd.Kfz. 251/6 Ausf. B painted in yellow or tan desert camouflage is positioned next to an armored van in North Africa. The head of a crewman wearing a white cap and goggles is visible next to the MG 34 on the forward gun mount.

At a site near Bir es Sfiri, Libya, in May 1942, an Sd.Kfz. 251/6 Ausf. B is set up for the use of a *Flieg-erverbindungsoffizier,* or aircraft liaison officer. These officers, nicknamed "flivos," were forward air controllers, who called in air-strikes on enemy positions on the ground. In addition to the frame antenna, a winch mast is fitted to the right rear of the vehicle.

Two Sd.Kfz. 251/6 command vehicles configured for flivo operations are operating in mountainous terrain. Both vehicles are equipped with winch masts; note the star antenna on the farther vehicle. The closer vehicle is an Ausf. B.

An Sd.Kfz. 251/6 flying a command pennant advances along a dusty road, most likely during the 1941 invasion of the Soviet Union. The command pennant design is repeated on the left fender. The letter *G* on the right fender signifies Panzergruppe Guderian. A roll of wire is stored on the front of the vehicle. Seven steel helmets are lined up along the upper part of the body. Note the drum magazine on the side of the MG 34. Two jerry can liquid containers are on the right fender. *Thomas Anderson collection*

Operators wearing tropical uniforms are at work in a radio-equipped Sd.Kfz. 251. The man in the foreground is wearing an aviator's helmet with headphones built in, while the next two men are wearing headphone sets. In the background on a swing arm is an MG 34. At the bottom of the photo are the front visors.

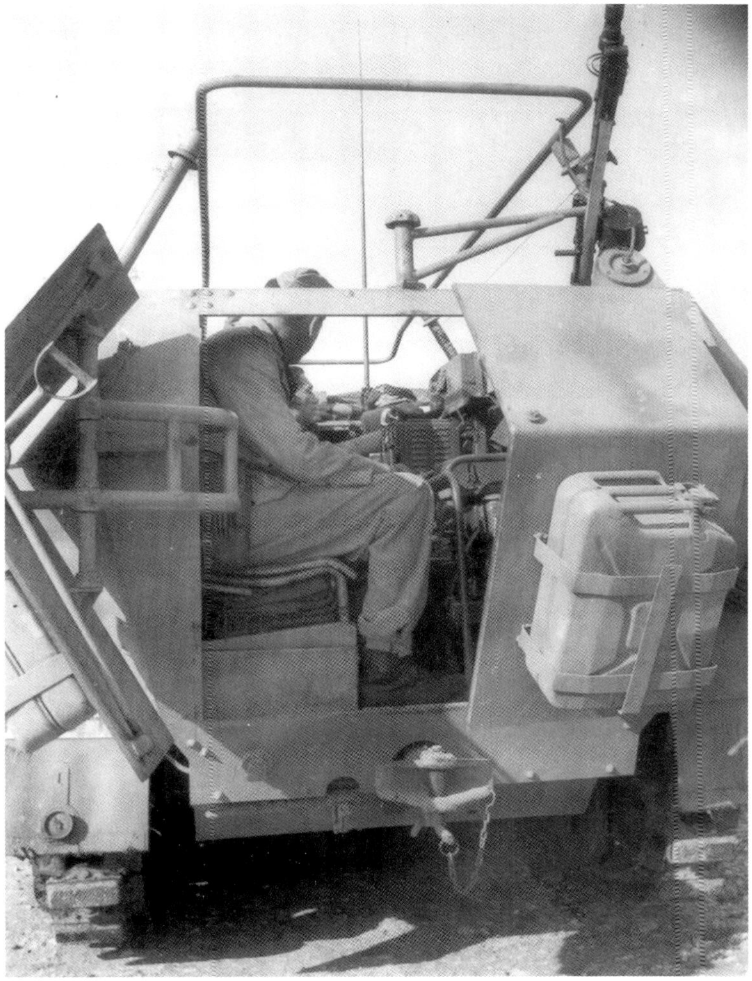

This may well be the same Sd.Kfz. 251 shown in the preceding photograph. The frame antenna is not the typical style found on Sd.Kfz. 251/6s. At the forward end of the compartment is a mast antenna. On the upper rear of the vehicle, below the ammunition drum for the MG 34, is a connection box for the cable running up to the frame mast.

Generaloberst Hermann Hoth, *right*, greets an officer alongside an Sd.Kfz. 251/6 Ausf. B on the southern front of the Soviet Union between the Don River and Stalingrad in the summer of 1942. A good view is available of the lower part of a winch mast on the rear of the vehicle. A dustcover is over the lowered top of the mast. *BA 218-0530-06*

This radio or command Sd.Kfz. 251 was based on an Ausf. A or Ausf. B chassis and body; the packs and equipment stored on the side of the body cover the presence or absence of visors that would differentiate between the two models. This frame antenna lacks the longitudinal center element and lateral elements seen on many Sd.Kfz. 251/6 frame antennas. Two jerry cans are stored on their sides on the rear of the fender. The nickname "Fuchs" is painted on the body to the rear of the driver's side visor.

The frame antenna on this Sd.Kfz. 251 Ausf. B command or radio vehicle has wire looped back and forth across it, presumably for enhanced range. Also, a rod antenna is mounted on the right rear of the body. The machine gun is wrapped with cloth to keep out dust.

The Sd.Kfz. 251/6 Ausf. A in the foreground is part of the 7th Panzer Division, and several Pz.Kpfw. 38(t) light tanks can be seen in the background advancing with it on June 10, 1940. This vehicle is the mount of the division commander at the time, Major General Erwin Rommel. The division had just broken out of the Somme bridgehead and is rapidly advancing toward the coast. The door on the side of the hood is open for ventilation purposes. A shovel and wire cutters are secured to the body toward the rear.

Several GIs confer next to a damaged Sd.Kfz. 251 Ausf. C with a high-frequency frame antenna. It's not clear what the purpose of the bent structure over and to the front of the cab was. Variations in *Rahmenantennen* (frame antennas) were present on the Sd.Kfz. 251 radio and command vehicles; this one has a flat surface with cross elements and extra longitudinal elements. It's not clear if this was an Sd.Kfz. 251/6 command vehicle or simply an improvised radio or command vehicle.

An Sd.Kfz. 251/6 Ausf. C drives past farm buildings on the eastern front. The vehicle has received a camouflage paint application that appears on close inspection to have been sprayed on. On the front plate of the body next to the license plate is the tactical symbol for a corps headquarters: two white triangles and two black or dark-colored triangles.

While personnel wait in a trench alongside a road, a senior officer to the rear of an MG 34 in an Sd.Kfz. 251/6 Ausf. C scans the ground ahead through binoculars. A removable ladder is attached to the side of the personnel compartment. Painted in white below the assistant driver's side visor is "P2." *Thomas Anderson collection*

During the invasion of Greece in April 1941, command staff of the 2nd Panzer Division pause to confer with civil and military personnel. Holding on to the top edge of the Sd.Kfz. 251/6 Ausf. A is Generalleutnant (lieutenant general) Rudolf Veiel, commander of the division at that time. An axe and a pick are clamped to the body. *BA 161-0257-16A*

Troops in an Sd.Kfz. 251/6 Ausf. D stop to confer with a soldier along a road in the Soviet Union in early 1944. The frame antenna on the vehicle is a real curiosity; it was one designed for use on the Sd.Kfz. 232 heavy armored reconnaissance vehicle. Notice the curve to the frame and the structure to the right that would have pivoted on a bearing above the Sd.Kfz. 232 turret. Mud has been brushed onto the vehicle to tone down the whitewash camouflage. *BA 693-0286-03A*

Sd.Kfz. 251/7

The Sd.Kfz. 251/7 was designed for use by the *Panzer Pionier Kompanie* (armored engineer company). In addition to carrying equipment particular to the armored engineers, the Sd.Kfz. 251/7 was outfitted with four brackets, two on each side, for transporting two treadway bridge sections with a capacity of 8 metric tons, or 8.8 tons. These bridges were sufficient for spanning trenches and small streams. This vehicle, an Ausf. C, license number WH-1384965, has "*Elch* (moose)/ 2" painted on the ventilator cowl and is towing a 2.8 cm *schwere Panzerbüchse 41* light antitank gun.

Photographed in a factory setting, this Sd.Kfz. 251/7 Ausf. C apparently was newly completed. The number "8" is marked on the side of the treadway bridge section. Each Sd.Kfz. 251/7 in a platoon was armed with two MG 34s. The shield and the barrel of the forward MG 34 are faintly visible in this photo.

Before the Sd.Kfz. 251/7 was introduced, *Pionier-Bataillon* 62 experimented with two Sd.Kfz. 251s with different arrangements for carrying engineer equipment. The tests commenced in May 1939. The vehicle shown here is configured in the manner that the battalion recommended for vehicles 1, 3, and 5 in each engineer platoon. In the front of the personnel compartment is a large roll of wire; to the rear of the seated men are, *left*, various cases for equipment, and, *right*, a reel of wire.

The interior of the same Sd.Kfz. 251 test vehicle as proposed for vehicles 1, 3, and 5 of an engineer platoon is viewed from above. The hinged seats are raised, showing the equipment stowed below the seats. This vehicle was designed to carry a total of 1,173 pounds of engineer equipment.

The interior of an Sd.Kfz. 251 test vehicle configured for vehicles 2, 4, and 6 of a Wehrmacht engineer platoon is shown in a photo taken around May 1939. This vehicle was intended to carry 1,074 pounds of engineer equipment: 99 pounds less than the vehicle for platoons 1, 3, and 5 of an engineer platoon. Along the left side are crates marked "*Sprengmittelkasten*" (explosives box).

As seen through the open doors, six engineer soldiers sit inside an Sd.Kfz. 251 test vehicle, as proposed by *Pionier-Bataillon* 62 for vehicles 2, 4, and 6 of an engineer platoon. Instead of the reel of wire that was in the right rear of the personnel compartment of the vehicle intended for platoons 1, 3, and 5, this vehicle had equipment cases in that spot.

Vehicle number "7" in an engineer platoon was to have been packed as demonstrated in this photo taken during *Pionier-Bataillon* 62's tests in 1939. The specified equipment weighed 1,642 pounds, and its arrangement presumably would have forced personnel to enter the vehicle by crawling over the boxes at the rear of the compartment or climbing over the sides of the body.

The same load for vehicle number "7" of an engineer platoon shown in the preceding photograph is viewed from above, facing the rear of the Sd.Kfz. 251. In the lower right is what appears to be a small generator or compressor.

The interior of an Sd.Kfz. 251/7 Ausf. C is viewed from above, with the rear of the vehicle toward the left. At the top is a treadway bridge section. To the right is the left bench seat. To the left are rope and ammunition boxes for the machine guns.

Faintly visible on the ventilation cowl to the side of the hood on Sd.Kfz. 251/7 Ausf. C with license number WG-1263298 is a nickname, most likely *Büffel* (Buffalo). Below the nickname is the numeral "1." A whip antenna is mounted on the inboard side of the right treadway bridge section.

An Sd.Kfz. 251/7 Ausf. C is being driven up an embankment during training maneuvers in Holland. "*Elch*" (Moose) with the number "2" below it is painted on the ventilation cowl. The number 24 is painted on the side of the treadway bridge. Clearly visible on the rear of the body is the tactical sign for an armored engineer company, with the number 3 next to it signifying the 3rd Company.

The same Sd.Kfz. 251/7 Ausf. C is seen, this time with the crew wearing caps instead of helmets, negotiating an embankment during training. The vehicle is towing a 2.8 cm *schwere Panzerbüchse* 41 (s.Pz.B. 41) squeeze-bore antitank gun, a weapon that was effective against many of the lightly armored vehicles of the early days of World War II.

An Sd.Kfz. 251/7 proceeds along a dock area in Port-Vendres in southern France during 1942. A short section of spare track links is propped up on the front fender. This vehicle was part of the 7th Panzer Division's motorized pioneers. On the front of the hull is the "Y" symbol of the 7th Panzer Division from 1941 to 1945. *BA 258-1320-10*

At a port in the South of France in 1942, several Sd.Kfz. 251/7s with treadway bridge sections loaded and troops aboard proceed toward the docks. Note the round lightening holes in the brackets that support the bridge sections. *BA 258-1320-07*

The crew of the first vehicle in a line of Sd.Kfz. 251/7 engineer vehicles smile for the photographer. At least the first two vehicles are Ausf. Ds; the third one may have been an Ausf. C. The half-tracks and the sides of the treadway bridges have a lightly streaked camouflage pattern. Brand-new-looking jerry cans are stowed on the nearest vehicle. *Tank Museum*

Crewmen are aboard these four Sd.Kfz. 251/7s with treadway bridges that are secured to railroad flatcars for long-distance transportation. Chocks were snugged up to the front and rear of the tires and the front and the rear of the track assemblies and then nailed securely to the floor of the flatcar.

Only the front ends of the treadway bridges betray this well-camouflaged vehicle as an Sd.Kfz. 251/7. A well-defined tactical symbol for an armored engineer company with a number "1" is on the frontal plate of the body; at the center of that plate is a very faint license number, marked in black, with a black border. *Thomas Anderson collection*

The treadway bridge sections are not present on this Sd.Kfz. 251/7. Blackout covers with small slits are fitted on the service headlights. Tree branches are arranged on the body of the vehicle for camouflage. Two men are faintly visible behind the machine gun shield.

On this Sd.Kfz. 251/7 Ausf. D, the space between the brackets on the left side for transporting a treadway bridge section has been filled in with wooden planks, making for a stowage bin. A saw and some steel cable are visible in the bin. An interesting insignia device is on the middle storage bin door and on the left side of the rear of the vehicle: a dark-colored rectangle with the insignia of the 20th Panzer Division; the lettering "Pz Pi 92," for *Panzer-Pionier-Bataillon* 92; and, *at the bottom*, the tactical sign for *Panzer-Pionier-Kompanie* 3. The number "302" refers to the assistant commander's vehicle of the 3rd Company. *BA 715-0212A-27A*

Sd.Kfz. 251/8

The German armed forces developed an armored ambulance designated the Sd.Kfz. 251/8 *mittlere Krankenpanzerwagen*. The vehicle could transport three stretcher patients or up to eight ambulatory patients. Here, an Sd.Kfz. 251/8 with a red-cross flag on the front passes a group of refugees on the western front in 1944. *BA 585-2194-17A*

All four submodels of the Sd.Kfz. 251, from Ausf. A to Ausf. D, were used for the Sd.Kfz. 251/8 *mittlere Krankenpanzerwagen*, such as this Ausf. D vehicle assigned to Panzer-Division "Hermann Göring," seen at the Monte Cassino area in Italy in 1944. A red-cross banner is on a rigid frame at the front of the personnel compartment, and a soldier is holding a red-cross flag. *BA 580-1989-10*

British troops inspect a captured Sd.Kfz. 251/8 Ausf. D. Except for the red-cross markings, the vehicle looked from the outside like any other medium *Schützenpanzerwagen*. Bows are installed over the personnel compartment, and at the rear is a rolled-up tarpaulin. *Tank Museum*

The interior of an Sd.Kfz. 251/8 is viewed through the rear door. Two metal tubes mounted crosswise on the top of the body, at the front and the rear of the personnel compartment, were fitted with chains that supported the inboard sides of the right and left upper stretcher holders. One such stretcher is shown resting on the right holders. A third stretcher patient was carried by swinging up the hinged right bench seat and placing the stretcher on holders on the floor, as seen here. *Tank Museum*

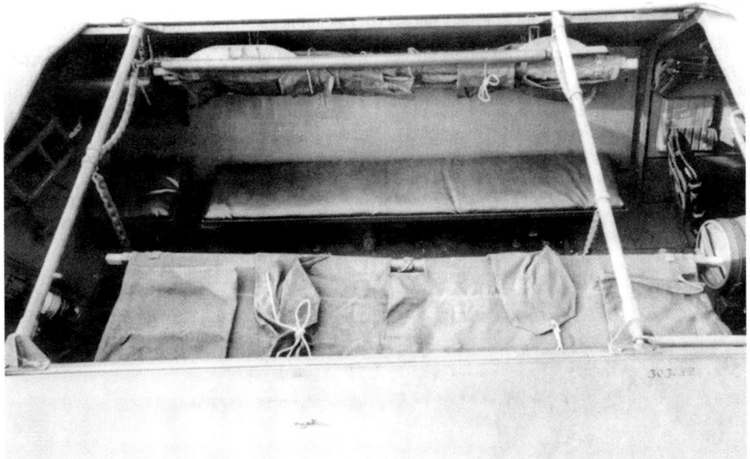

An Sd.Kfz. 251/8 is viewed from above the right side, showing a stretcher installed on the upper right position. The two cross-tubes with chains to support the inboard sides of two stretcher holders are visible. The lower ends of the chains were attached to the tubes when not in use. The outboard sides of the stretcher holders were mounted on the body, and when not in use the holders were collapsed and stored against the body.

Another view of the interior of an Sd.Kfz. 251/8 shows two stretchers on their holders on the right side of the compartment, and a seat for a single passenger folded down at the right rear of the compartment. At the front of the compartment between the driver's and the assistant driver's seats is a water cask.

The Sd.Kfz. 251/9, also designated *mittlerer Schützenpanzerwagen* (7.5 cm Kanone), was developed by the *Waffenamt* (Ordnance Department) and Büssing-NAG in early 1942. It mounted the 7.5 cm Kanone 37 L/24, a weapon previously used on the *Sturmgeschütz*. Initially, the gun protruded through a cutout in the right side of the frontal plate of the cab.

In a gunner's-view photograph of the 7.5 cm Kanone 37 L/24 in an Sd.Kfz. 251/9, to the left is the Sfl.Z.F.1 periscopic sight. At the upper center is the breech, to the rear of which is the recoil shield. Below that shield is a collection bin for spent casings. At the lower center is the gunner's seat and its tubular support arm.

An overall view of an Sd.Kfz. 251/9 from above shows the relative positions of the 7.5 cm Kanone L/24, the gun shield, the gunner's seat, the bench seat in the right rear of the compartment, and the ammunition locker in the left rear of the compartment. The vehicle had a carrying capacity of thirty-two rounds of 7.5 cm ammunition, consisting of a mix of high-explosive and shaped-charge rounds.

The crew of an Sd.Kfz. 251/9 on the eastern front, including one to the rear with a scissors periscope, scan the terrain ahead for signs of enemy emplacements. (The Teleplast 10× *Handscherenfernrohr* binocular "scissors" periscope was a standard piece of equipment in the Sd.Kfz. 251/9.) Remnants of whitewashed camouflage, most of which has washed off, are on the vehicle. Metal strips in the shape of a *T* have been fastened to the dip in the fender, to form a stowage bin. *Thomas Anderson collection*

An Allied soldier inspects a captured *Sturmgeschütz* III assault gun parked next to an Sd.Kfz. 251/9 with 7.5 cm Kanone 37 L/24. The number 1144 is marked on the hull. The front of the fender is badly crumpled. Lying on the ground between the two vehicles is a *Panzerfaust* recoilless antitank weapon. *Patton Museum*

This Sd.Kfz. 251/9, photographed after being captured by the Allies at Normandy, bears the trident insignia used by the 2nd Panzer Division from 1943 to 1945. Below it is the tactical sign for an armored car company, number "5," and it is reported that this vehicle was assigned to 5 Panzerspähwagen Kompanie. An illegible nickname is painted above the driver's side vision slit, and a shipping label is below the slit. *Patton Museum*

The same captured Sd.Kfz. 251/9 seen in the preceding photograph is shown in another image, this time with the paint and markings in a deteriorated condition. Whereas the front storage compartment door in the preceding photo was visibly dented, the door in this photo seems to be undamaged. A turnbuckle and shackle, probably for use in transporting the vehicle, is lying on the side of the hood. *Patton Museum*

An Sd.Kfz. 251/9 Ausf. C climbs a long grade in advance of a column of vehicles in the distance. A rod antenna is mounted on the left side of the body, and spare tracks are fastened to the front plate of the body. The vehicle has a camouflage paint pattern; a black-and-white *Balkenkreuz* is on the doors of the hood.

In a column of vehicles crossing a steppe on the southern front in the USSR in January 1944, an Sd.Kfz. 251/9 Ausf. D is in the foreground, with three more Sd.Kfz. 251s following. The only marking visible on the lead vehicle is the license plate, which is obscured by mud. *BA 711-0410-33*

Among the vehicles of a German column passing through a small settlement on the eastern front in the summer of 1944 is an Sd.Kfz. 251/9 Ausf. D (*toward the left*). This vehicle had the 7.5 cm Kanone 51 L/24, introduced to the 251/9 after the 630th vehicle produced. Superseding the 7.5 cm Kanone 37, the 7.5 cm Kanone 51 was mounted above the top of the body of the vehicle and had a new armored structure to the front and sides of the mount. *BA 696-0438-06*

The higher position of the 7.5 cm Kanone 51 L/24 on the Sd.Kfz. 251/9 is apparent from this angle. Now the gun was centered above the cab, instead of offset to the right side, as was the case with the 7.5 cm Kanone 37 L/24. This version of the 251/9 also featured an MG 42 to the right of the 7.5 cm gun; it is visible here above the frontal shield.

An abandoned Sd.Kfz. 251/9 with 7.5 cm Kanone 51 L/24 is seen from above. Both of the side shields are shattered, and the MG 42 has been wrenched from its mount. Inside the fighting compartment are tarpaulins and a mass of clutter. A rifle lies on top of the 7.5 cm ammunition box. As in the majority of photos of knocked-out Sd.Kfz. 251 Ausf. Ds, all the storage compartment doors are open.

A GI inspects a captured Sd.Kfz. 251/9 with 7.5 cm Kanone 51 L/24. Stenciled on the side of the sleeve of the 7.5 cm gun is "braun-ark," which refers to the type of lubricant to be used in the gun's recoil and recuperator systems. The hood doors are missing. In the background is an Sd.Kfz. 251/21 Ausf D with "*Drilling*."

Photographed while on display at the Patton Museum of Cavalry and Armor, Fort Knox, Kentucky, this late Sd.Kfz. 251/9 had been with Panzeraufklarungs-Abteilung 20, 20th Panzer Division, when its crew surrendered it to US forces in late April or early May 1945. *Don Moriarty*

The Sd.Kfz. 251/9 came to Fort Knox in 1946 and was displayed for decades outdoors. Although the camouflage paint is a nonoriginal simulation, the vehicle has a replica of its original license plate number, WH-1808565. The vehicle also bears its original tactical number, 417. *Don Moriarty*

Below the license plate is the round cover for the engine manual-starting crank. The front of the body of the Sd.Kfz. 250/9 encloses the engine compartment. The disk-shaped object to the front of the engine compartment doors is the armored cover for the radiator filler. *Don Moriarty*

The Sd.Kfz. 251/9 mounted 7.25-20 tires with directional treads. The tires on this vehicle are not original pattern but are the same style used on the OT-810, a postwar copy of the Sd.Kfz. 251 Ausf. D produced by the Czechoslovakians. *Don Moriarty*

Arrayed along the lower panels of the upper bodywork are three storage compartments, each with its own flush-fitted door. Above the vehicular data stencil over the front door is the driver's side vision slit. *Don Moriarty*

The radio antenna mount is a welded assembly that hooks over the top of the left side of the body. To the rear of it is a lifting eye for the upper hull.

To the left of the tow pintle at the rear of the vehicle is the compressed-air coupling and shutoff valve for a trailer connection. Above the valve is an electrical socket.

Above the license plate is the Notek blackout taillight. The design of the stamped-steel Zpw. 5001/280/140 tracks is visible. This track was introduced as a result of the rubber shortage, which hindered production of the cast Zgw. 5001/280/140 track, which featured rubber blocks. *Don Moriarty*

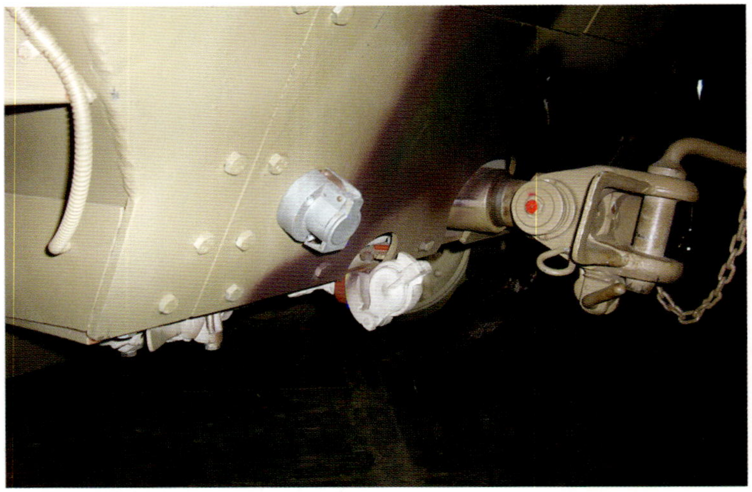

The electric socket, compressed-air coupling, and tow pintle with its retainer chain are viewed from the side. *Don Moriarty*

Viewed from below is the compressed-air coupling (*right*), with the air shutoff valve to the left. *Don Moriarty*

A view from the left rear corner of the crew compartment shows the welded and bolted construction of the plates. *Don Moriarty*

The upper bodywork at the right rear of the Sd.Kfz. 251/9 is highlighted. At the lower center, the upper side of the top hinge of the rear door is visible. *Don Moriarty*

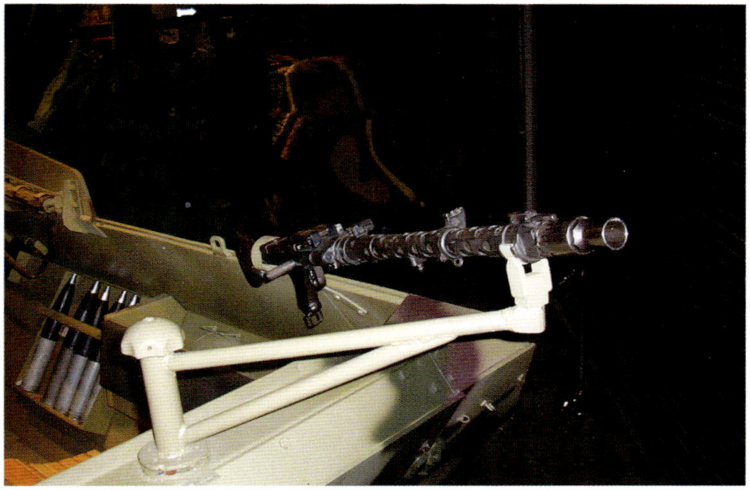

An MG 34 is in a stowed configuration. The tubular welded construction of the pivoting machine gun mount is shown. *Don Moriarty*

Clamped to the buttstock of the MG 34 is a travel lock mounted on an arm fastened to the vehicle's body. *Don Moriarty*

A view into the rear of the fighting compartment shows a fire extinguisher with a Tetra label; these were typically painted a less conspicuous color such as gray or *Dunkelgelb. Don Moriarty*

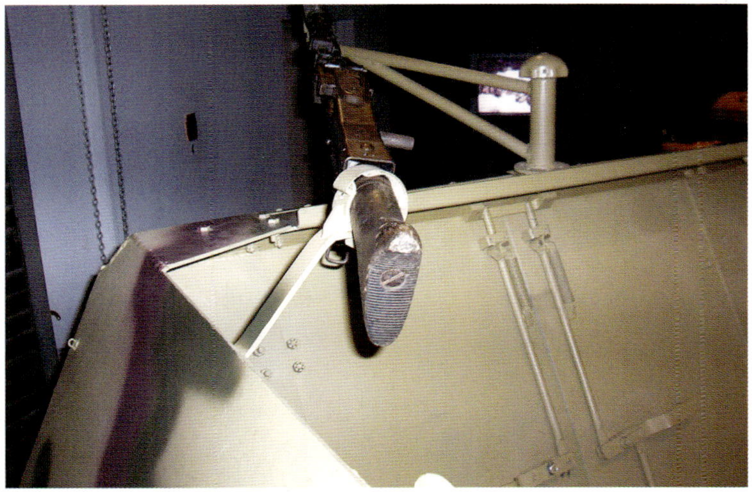

The machine gun mount, travel lock, and details of the insides of the rear doors and locking mechanisms are in view. *Don Moriarty*

The engine compartment doors, viewed from the left side, are flush-mounted, with two exterior hinges each. Visible in the foreground is the weld seam between the top and side body plates. *Don Moriarty*

On the inner side of the driver's visor are the operating arms as well as the housing for a glass vision block. Visible inside the top of the port is the driver's forehead pad. *Don Moriarty*

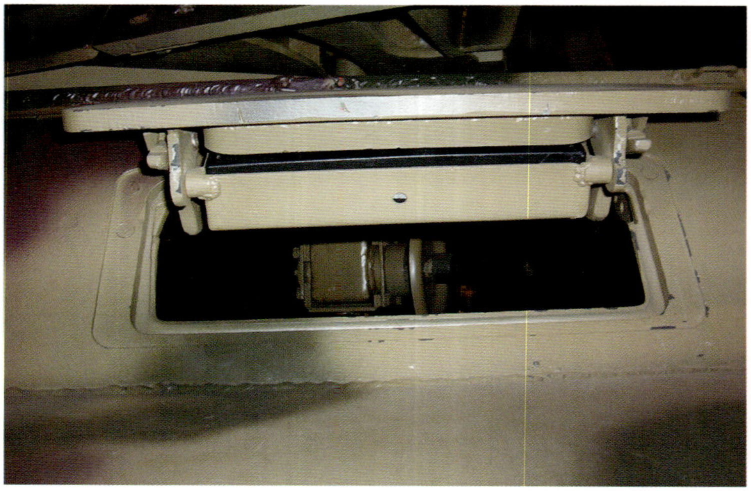

The vision ports on this Sd.Kfz. 251/9 are of the late flat style, simplified from the earlier style with the protruding front surface around the vision slit. *Don Moriarty*

The driver's vision port is viewed from the left side, also showing the front left corner of the armored superstructure and, *at top center*, the side of the gun shield. *Don Moriarty*

The forward elements of the 7.5 cm Kanone 51 (Sf) installation include, *left to right*, the barrel (note the rifling), barrel shield, and box-shaped mantlet. *Don Moriarty*

The mantlet consists of a frontal plate bolted to a welded box with an angled shield, to the rear of which is a larger, angled shield that traverses in unison with the gun. *Don Moriarty*

Traverse of the main gun of the late-model Sd.Kfz. 251/9 was 20 degrees to each side of center, an improvement over the 10 degrees left and 12 degrees right of the early gun mount. *Don Moriarty*

For the Sd.Kfz. 251/9, the section leader's seat to the right of the driver's seat was eliminated. A plain, nonopening armored plate replaced the front visor. *Don Moriarty*

The loop at the bottom front of the barrel shield was for attaching a gun cover. The rifling of the gun includes twenty-eight grooves. *Don Moriarty*

The 7.5 cm Kanone 51 (Sf) is mounted on an armor plate bolted over the driver's compartment. Note the loops welded to the front edge of that plate. *Don Moriarty*

Viewing across the gun mount from the left, in the foreground is the gunner's periscopic sight. Beyond the breech of the 7.5 cm gun is an MG 42 machine gun. *Don Moriarty*

A closer view of the breech (*upper right*) and recoil guard of the 7.5 cm Kanone 51 (Sf), with the left trunnion to the lower left. Gun elevation was –10 degrees to +16 degrees. *Don Moriarty*

The gunner's sight in the Sd.Kfz. 251/9 was the *Selbstfahrlafetten-Zielfernrohr* 1 (Sfl.Z.F. 1), a periscopic sight used on several other German vehicles and artillery pieces. *Don Moriarty*

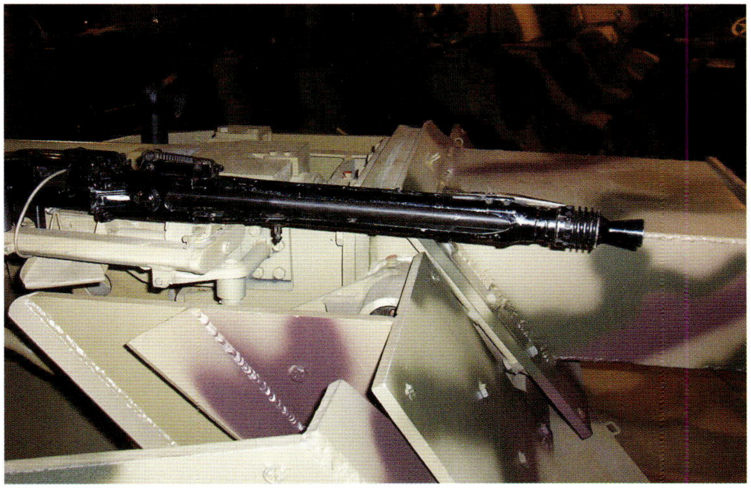

To the right side of the 7.5 cm gun mount is an MG 42 7.92 mm machine gun attached to a lafette, or gun carriage, which elevates and traverses in unison with the main gun. *Don Moriarty*

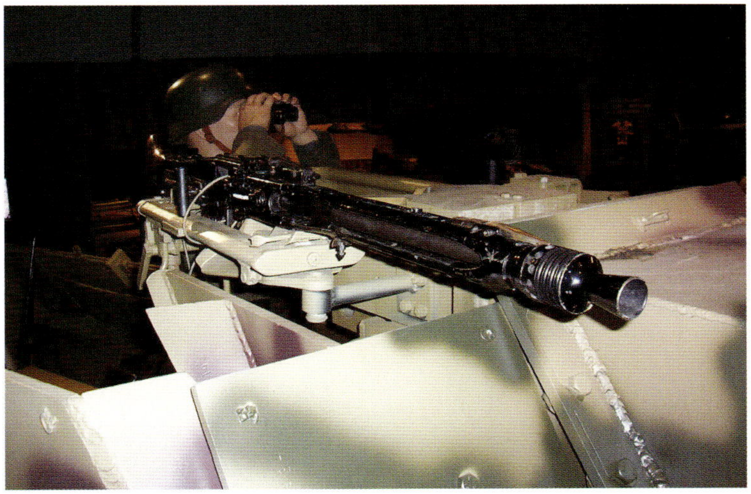

A horizontal post bolted to the side of the gun mount supports the front of the lafette. The MG 42 and lafette could be installed on a tripod mount for use away from the vehicle. *Don Moriarty*

The eyepiece and forehead guard of the Sfl.Z.F.1 gunsight are shown close-up. To the upper right is the breech of the 7.5 cm gun. *Don Moriarty*

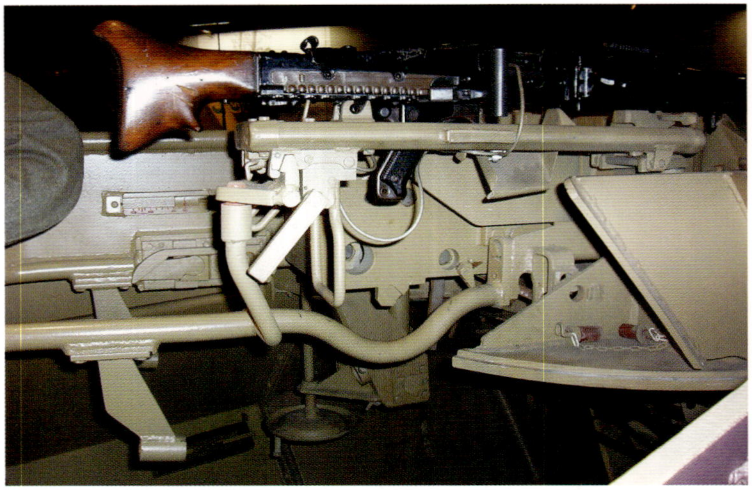

The right side of the MG 42 and the lafette are in view, as well as the inboard face of the recoil guard of the 7.5 cm gun (*left*) and tubing supporting the recoil guard. *Don Moriarty*

The ready rack has a hinged retainer secured on the right side by a half wing nut. Note the diamond tread pattern on the removable floor plates. *Don Moriarty*

In late Sd.Kfz. 251/9s, wooden-slat seats replaced the earlier upholstered seats. This wooden seat is a recent reproduction. A backrest is on the stowage bin. *Don Moriarty*

The bench seat is attached to the lid of a storage box with three hinges. On the seat are two 7.92 mm ammunition boxes. *Don Moriarty*

Sd.Kfz. 251/10

The Sd.Kfz. 251/10, or *mittlerer Schützenpanzerwagen* (3.7 cm Pak 36), entered production in mid-1941 and saw use in the infantry-support role, with the 3.7 cm gun able to engage infantry concentrations, soft-skin vehicles, and the lightly armored vehicles of the early stages of World War II. The example shown here was based on an Ausf. C vehicle. *Walter J. Spielberger collection*

The same Sd.Kfz. 251/10 is observed from the left side. To the left side of the 3.7 cm gun was a shield for the protection of the gunner. The shield consisted of spaced armor. To the rear of the gun breech is a recoil guard, to shield the gunner from injury when the gun was fired. *Walter J. Spielberger collection*

The crew of an Sd.Kfz. 251/10 pose with their weapon; this type of vehicle was specified as having a crew of six. On the left side of the 3.7 cm gun is the gunsight and the aperture for it in the armored shield. The recoil shield on the left side of the gun breech had a curve at the rear, ostensibly for stopping ejected spent cartridge cases. *BA 217-0493-27*

Although the 3.7 mm Pak of the Sd.Kfz. 251/10 was outdated by the time the vehicle went into production and packed less of a punch than the 7.5 cm Kanone, the weapon still could defeat moderate thicknesses of armor at close ranges, and it packed a respectable punch when used against infantry positions. Provisions for storing 168 rounds of 3.7 cm ammunition were in the vehicle. *Walter J. Spielberger collection*

A soldier, possibly the commander of this Sd.Kfz. 251/10, poses for the photographer. This vehicle is evidence of the condition that a coat of winter-camouflage whitewash would deteriorate to after weeks or months in the elements. Two jerry cans are secured with straps to the rear of the body. *Thomas Anderson collection*

In the spring of 1944, an Sd.Kfz. 251/10 pauses near a knocked-out Soviet Sherman tank on the eastern front. A bundle of sticks is on the front of the half-track, and the vehicle has white-wash camouflage. The vehicle is missing the fronts of its fenders. *BA 090-3918-03*

A medic stops to talk to the crew of an Sd.Kfz. 251/10 as one of the members scans to the distance through binoculars. The crewmen are wearing camouflage smocks as well as camouflage helmet covers and a similarly appointed *Feldmütze* (field cap). A wooden beam is secured to the side of the body with wires; it likely was an unditching beam, for aiding the tires and tracks to gain traction when mired in mud.

Members of the crew of an Sd.Kfz. 251/10 Ausf. C observe a heavy bombardment in the distance. The body of the half-track has a roughly applied camouflage scheme to enable the vehicle to blend in with the local terrain. The Sd.Kfz. 251/10s often were assigned to platoon leaders in panzer-grenadier companies.

Crewmen in parkas riding in an Sd.Kfz. 251/10 Ausf. C include a very young-looking one in the middle. The original dark base color of the vehicle is visible around the front visors, where whitewash was not applied. A German flag with swastika is lashed to the hood as a recognition aid for friendly aerial forces. Steel helmets are stowed to the rear of the rod antenna. *Thomas Anderson collection*

In addition to the purpose-built Sd.Kfz. 251/10s, with factory-installed 3.7 cm guns, numerous Sd.Kfz. 251s were fitted with the guns, cradles, and shields of towed 3.7 cm Pak 36s, possibly as early as 1940, before the Sd.Kfz. 251/10 entered production. This Sd.Kfz. 251 Ausf. B with an extemporized 3.7 cm Pak 36 mount has an inverted number "3" by the tactical sign.

A British soldier is at the controls of the 3.7 cm Pak 36 on this Sd.Kfz. 251 Ausf. B captured in North Africa. Since these conversions appear to have been field modifications, the designs of the mounts varied from unit to unit. This gun is mounted on a box-shaped base on the cab roof, giving the gun a higher position than the one in the preceding photo. *Patton Museum*

In another photo of the captured Sd.Kfz. 251 Ausf. B, the Tommy has his left hand on the traversing handwheel of the 3.7 cm Pak 36. Above that handwheel is the elevating handwheel, with the left firing plunger in the center of it. The telescopic gunsight is above the elevating wheel. Note the opening on the side of the body where a projectile passed through it, and the buckled armor along the welded joint adjacent to the hole. *Walter J. Spielberger collection*

An Sd.Kfz. 251 with a 3.7 cm Pak 36 is part of a convoy passing through a settlement. This is an Ausf. A vehicle, as indicated by the visor to the rear of the *Balkenkreuz*. A bundle of stakes is lashed to the front of the vehicle.

Sd.Kfz. 251/11

The Sd.Kfz. 251/11 *mittlerer Fernsprechpanzerwagen* was a field-telephone vehicle, equipped with a telephone switchboard and the means for running telephone lines. Visible on this Ausf. C example are a cable reel and holder on the right fender, a reel holder in the rear of the personnel compartment, and a machine gun with a cover and shield on the cab roof. The officer in the rear of the vehicle is holding a wire pike, a lineman tool consisting of a wooden pole with a hook and roller on the end, for laying paid-out telephone lines to the side of the road, or for recovering lines. *Patton Museum*

This is a field-telephone switchboard in an Sd.Kfz. 251/11, with two cable-reel holders on top of its cabinet, one with a reel installed. To the front and the rear of the switchboard cabinet are parts bins. *Tank Museum*

Sd.Kfz. 251/16

To give its troops a mobile, armored flamethrower capability, the Wehrmacht ordered the development of the Sd.Kfz. 251/16 *mittlerer Flammpanzerwagen*. This was armed with two 1.4 cm *Strahlrohren* (projector tubes) on pivoting mounts with armor shields converted from machine gun shields, with one mount on the upper part of the body on each side of the personnel compartment. In addition, a handheld 0.7 cm flamethrower with extension hoses was available for use away from the vehicle; this equipment is stored on the rear of this Ausf. C vehicle. *Patton Museum*

The two 1.4 cm flamethrowers were staggered, with the one on the right side more forward. Flexible hoses conducted flame oil from two tanks in the rear of the compartment to the flamethrowers. Each flamethrower had a lever for aiming the weapon, with a trigger lever below the handle. To the front is an MG 34 and armored shield.

An early-type 1.4 cm flamethrower is viewed from outside of an Sd.Kfz. 251/16. Note the wedge-shaped mounting bracket for the flamethrower mount, and the coil-spring counterbalance above the mounting bracket. The flame oil of the 1.4 cm flamethrowers was ignited by electrically igniting a charge of gasoline, while the handheld 0.7 cm flamethrower was ignited by a blank cartridge.

Two operators in camouflage suits, including one with a face mask and goggles, stand next to the flamethrowers in an Sd.Kfz. 251/16. Note the bottle-shaped slot in the center of the flamethrower shield, and the flame oil spattered on the vehicle body. *Walter J. Spielberger collection*

With the rear doors open, a view is available of the interior of a knocked-out Sd.Kfz. 251/16 with early-type 1.4 cm flamethrowers. In addition to the two flame-oil tanks, there was a motor for driving a Koebe flamethrower pump. The flexible hoses have burned off or been removed from the flamethrowers. *Tank Museum*

Crewmen of an Sd.Kfz. 251/16 stand by, ready to send flames on an unfortunate target in a bombed-out village. This is an early-type 1.4 cm flamethrower and shield combination; at least two later types of flamethrower and shield combinations were introduced. *Walter J. Spielberger collection*

In a photo possibly related to the action depicted in the preceding photo, an Sd.Kfz. 251/16 Ausf. D with the vehicle number 644 on the side of the body and on the rear doors wreaks havoc with its 1.4 cm flamethrowers at a site on the central front in the Soviet Union. Combat experience proved that the handheld 0.7 cm flamethrower, which, with its hose, originally was stored on the rear of the vehicle when not in use, was not necessary, and it was deleted. *Walter J. Spielberger collection*

The last two digits of a vehicle number, "44," are visible on the rear doors of this Sd.Kfz. 251/16 Ausf. D, and it probably was the same vehicle as the one in the preceding photograph. The flamethrowers had a traverse of 160 degrees and could be depressed, as seen here, for close-in operation. The crew consisted of a commander / radio operator, two flamethrower gunners, and the driver. *Walter J. Spielberger collection*

Sd.Kfz. 251/20

The Germans began experimenting with military applications of infrared light for night-vision purposes in the mid-1930s. Late in World War II, they undertook a limited effort to mount infrared lighting and sighting devices on armored vehicles. One such vehicle was the Sd.Kfz. 251/20, also referred to as *mittlerer Schützenpanzerwagen ("Uhu,"* which is German for eagle-owl). The vehicle's infrared searchlights and sights were intended to be part of a system to illuminate the battlefield, working in conjunction with infrared-equipped Panther tanks. Seen here is a test example of an Sd.Kfz. 251/20.

The same test vehicle is seen from the right side. Key features of the Sd.Kfz. 251/20 were a 60 cm searchlight and, below it, an infrared sight, on a pedestal mount above the personnel compartment; a 20 cm infrared searchlight at the center of the frontal plate of the cab; and an FG 1252 infrared sight to the front of the driver's visor port. Special platforms were set up at the top of each side of the body of this test vehicle.

The powerful 60 cm infrared searchlight of the Sd.Kfz. 251/20 provided broad IR illumination of a battlefield. Below the searchlight is the infrared sight associated with the searchlight. A protective cover is fitted over the front of the sight.

With the rear doors of an Sd.Kfz. 251/20 Ausf. D open, the seating arrangement for the operator of the 60 cm infrared searchlight is visible. The pedestal containing the searchlight and the infrared sight, the operator's seat, and his controls are mounted on a turntable on the floor of the personnel compartment.

The operator's station for the 60 cm infrared searchlight is seen from a closer perspective. Toward the top center of the photo, below the crossbar below the searchlight, is the infrared sight, with a small eyepiece at the rear. Below the sight, to the right and left front of the seat, are handwheels for controlling the azimuth and elevation of the searchlight.

Some examples of the *mittlerer Schützenpanzerwagen (Uhu)* lacked the 60 cm infrared searchlight mount but were equipped with the driver's infrared searchlight and FG 1252 sight as well as an MG 42 with an FG 1250 infrared scope, as seen on this example photographed at the special training center for panzer troops at Fallingbostel, Germany, in March 1945. *Tank Museum*

The same *mittlerer Schützenpanzerwagen (Uhu)* shown in the preceding photo is viewed from a different angle, showing the infrared searchlight on the upper right of the MG 42 and the FG 1250 infrared scope on the upper left of the machine gun. On the side of the driver's compartment is a shipping label that includes the nomenclature of the vehicle, Sd.Kfz. 251/20. *Tank Museum*

A left-side view of the MG 42 and the infrared sight on an Sd.Kfz. 251/20 also includes a clear view of the shipping label stenciled below the driver's side vision slit. The data reads, *top to bottom*, Sd.Kfz. 251/20, *Leergew* (unloaded weight) 7.0 t (metric tons), *Nutzlast* (payload) 2.3 t, *Gesamtgew* (gross weight) 9.3 t, and V.Kl. (*Verladeklasse*: railroad classification number) Ib. The Ib class was specified for shipping vehicles with a weight up to 10 metric tons (11 US tons) and a length between 5.01 and 6.00 meters (16.44 feet to 19.7 feet). *Tank Museum*

A line of vehicles parked at the special training center for panzer troops at Fallingbostel, Germany, in March 1945 include several Sd.Kfz. 251/20s. This center gathered forces from several units to train them in night-fighting methods utilizing infrared equipment, a concept that was revolutionary for the time but is now an established facet of warfare. *Tank Museum*

The Sd.Kfz. 251/20 with the infrared-equipped MG 42 is viewed from the front right. The infrared sights would have given the driver a good chance of approaching an enemy concentration undetected and the gunner a good chance of getting early, accurate hits, but the muzzle flash of the gun eventually would have given away its location unless the vehicle kept under motion. Note the location of the radio antenna on the hood. *Tank Museum*

The interior and cab of an Sd.Kfz. 251/20 with infrared-equipped MG 42 are shown. The rear of the driver's infrared scope is visible through his open visor port. To the front of the assistant driver's seat is a radio set. This interior was photographed at the special training center for panzer troops at Fallingbostel, Germany, in March 1945. *Tank Museum*

Electrical boxes and cables related to the infrared searchlights and scopes of an Sd.Kfz. 251/20 are seen from the personnel compartment, with the assistant driver's seat to the center and the right side of the cab roof to the top. *Tank Museum*

Sd.Kfz. 251/21

Introduced in 1944, the Sd.Kfz. 251/21 featured a pedestal-mounted Drilling (triple) antiaircraft gun mount with an armored shield. The weapons were MG 151 1.5 cm automatic cannons, mounted side by side. The cannons were fed ammunition by belts from three magazines, with 250 rounds for the outboard cannons and 500 for the center one. However, the first 85 Sd.Kfz. 251/21s carried 3,000 rounds of 1.5 cm ammunition. Additional ammunition was stowed in bins in the vehicle.

The Drilling mount of the Sd.Kfz. 251/21 had an armor shield that protected the front and the sides. In addition, a four-sided armor shield was added to the top of the vehicle for added protection. The gunner traversed and elevated the guns by body motion; his seat was designed so that his body weight counterbalanced the front-heavy cannons. To the front of this gunner's face is the gunsight with padded eyepiece.

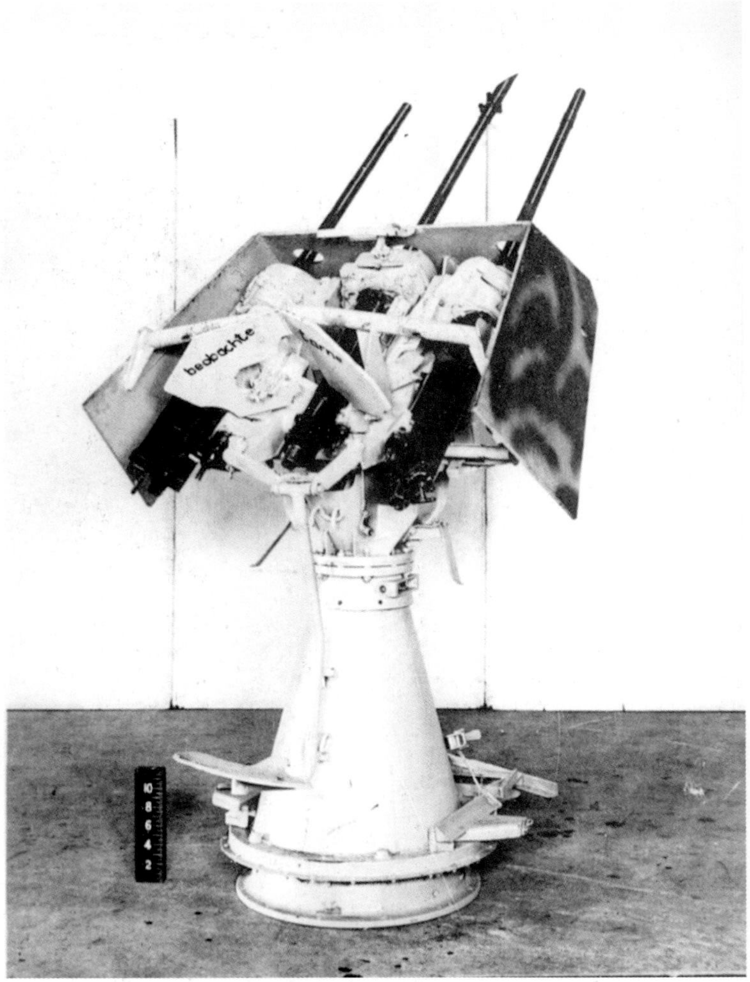

The Drilling MG 151 1.5 cm mount, including shield, cannons, cradle, pedestal, and gunner's seat, is shown removed from an Sd.Kfz. 251/21. The seat is attached to the rear of the gun cradle by a long arm. Above the receivers of the guns is a feature not seen in the preceding photo: a V-shaped facial shield.

Toward the end of World War II, victorious Soviet troops pose in and alongside a captured Sd.Kfz. 251/21. The vehicle has what appears to be a faded, sprayed-on camouflage scheme with random splotches of light-colored paint, such as on the side of the gun shield. The number "2" with a dot after it is on the side of the body. *Tank Museum*

Near the end of World War II, in the winter of 1944–45 an abandoned Sd.Kfz. 251/21 sits near a bombed-out building. Although these vehicles were not produced in large numbers, some of them saw action in the Battle of the Bulge and in the final battles in Germany. The muzzles of the outboard guns were fitted with flash suppressors with angled forward ends, while the center gun lacked a suppressor.

A knocked-out or abandoned Sd.Kfz. 251/21 on a road outside Saint-Vith, Belgium, in early 1945 bears a vehicle number on its side. The first digit is obscure but may be a "4," while the other two are "25." The rear panel of the armor mounted on top of the body is missing. The Drilling mount is traversed to the right side and elevated steeply.

A photographer with the 3rd Infantry Division photographed this destroyed Sd.Kfz. 251/21 Ausf. D amid the ruins of La Bourgance, France, on November 15, 1944. The Drilling gun mount is turned to the right side of the vehicle in this image. Visible above the armored side shield atop the vehicle's body are the rear of the face shield for the gunner and the rear of the gunner's sight, as well as parts of the side shields of the gun mount.

The corpse of a crewman of an Sd.Kfz. 251/21 lies in the ruins near Kientzheim, France, on December 21, 1944. The body of the vehicle to the rear of the cab is shattered, permitting a view of the right ammunition box below the Drilling shield. Between the receivers of the center and left guns is a telescopic gunsight with a rubber eyepiece.

Sd.Kfz. 251/22

The Sd.Kfz. 251/22, or *mittlerer Schützenpanzerwagen* (7.5 cm Pak), was developed in late 1944 as a mobile antitank gun and featured a 7.5 cm Pak 40 L/46 on a limited-traverse mount. The gun, upper carriage, traversing table, and shield were taken from a towed 7.5 cm Pak 40 and mounted on a special platform constructed at the front end of the personnel compartment of the vehicle.

At a battleground in the final days of the war, a knocked-out Sd.Kfz. 251/22 lies yards away from a destroyed Soviet T-34/85 tank. Incongruously, the fuselages of three German fighter planes are stacked upright behind the fence. The stenciled vehicle number 424 is on the side of the half-track. The right wheel and fender have been blown off. *Thomas Anderson collection*

Around the end of World War II, an Sd.Kfz. 251/22 rests with other Wehrmacht vehicles at a collection depot for captured German vehicles. Evidence indicates that this location probably was in Bohemia, or western Czechoslovakia. Very faintly visible to the right of the right rear door is the insignia of the 11th Panzer Division. The spaced armor of the gun shield is visible from this angle.

In another photo taken at the vehicle collection depot, the same Sd.Kfz. 251/22 is seen from the front, showing the license plate, WH-1810156. This vehicle had the late-type hood, with a single main door that was hinged at the rear, to the front of which, and extending to the front of the hood, was a smaller door, hinged on the right side. Note the travel lock for the 7.5 cm gun at the center of the cab roof. To the left is a Jagdpanzer 38 (Sd. Kfz. 138/2) Hetzer.

The interior of the same Sd.Kfz. 251/22 is viewed from the rear. The lower corners of the shield of the 7.5 cm Pak 40 were trimmed to prevent the shield from jamming on the top edges of the vehicle body. The raised platform with I-beam legs that supported the gun mount is visible. To the left are packing tubes for 7.5 cm rounds.

The 7.5 cm Pak 40 in a captured Sd.Kfz. 251/22 is seen from above, showing the guards to each side of the breech, the operating lever on top of the breech, the spaced-armor shield, the elevating and traversing handwheels, and other features. To the lower right of the gun mount is an ammunition storage box. This and the preceding several photos were taken by Ordnance Capt. D. M. Gilles for his intelligence report on German vehicles.

2 cm Flak 38 auf SPW

The 2 cm Flak 38 *auf Schützenpanzerwagen* was developed for the Luftwaffe as an armored, mobile antiaircraft vehicle. It was armed with the 2 cm Flak 38 automatic cannon. To provide clearance for the gun mount, a radical modification was made to the body of the vehicle, which comprised a bulged panel, hinged at the bottom, on each side. *Walter J. Spielberger collection*

The hinged body sections could be lowered when the 2 cm Flak 38 was placed in action, to allow more room for the gun and the crew to maneuver. Note the hinged arms at the front and the rear of the side panel, which acted to hold it in the lowered position. *Patton Museum*

This Sd.Kfz. 251 with a conversion body for a 2 cm Flak 38 has been repurposed to a radio or command vehicle with a frame antenna. Although the license plate is partially hidden by the tow cable, it is a Luftwaffe version. The officer is wearing the uniform of one of the "Hermann Göring" ground units, and the white circle with a diagonal line on it, on the front of the ventilation cowl, is consistent with a 10th Battery tactical symbol for the "Hermann Göring" ground units. *Walter J. Spielberger collection*

The layout of the multipaneled armored shield of the 2 cm Flak 38 *auf Schützenpanzerwagen* is visible from this angle in a view of a vehicle and crew of the 10th Battery, Flak-Regiment "Hermann Göring," during training in 1942. Behind the rear shield sits the gunner, while the loader stands to the left of the gun. This vehicle bore license number WL-174406. Note the number "7" below the side visor, the location of the storage box alongside the cab, and the case stored on top of the cab. *Patton Museum*

A "Hermann Göring" ground-unit symbol for a 10th Company is seen to good advantage on the left ventilation cowl of a 2 cm Flak 38 *auf Schützenpanzerwagen* negotiating a trail. Chicken wire is strung across the gun shields for the purpose of attaching tree branches, for camouflage. On the sides of the hood and the cab are standard-issue racks for Kar 98 rifles, three per side. *Patton Museum*

The crewmen are at their stations in a heavily camouflaged 2 cm Flak 38 *auf Schützenpanzerwagen*. The vehicle itself is camouflage painted, and local vegetation and tree branches add to the disguise. Visible in a gap in the foliage on the left rear door is a clock-face tactical sign for a 6th Company in a "Hermann Göring" ground unit. *Patton Museum*

This may be a view of the same 2 cm Flak 38 *auf Schützenpanzerwagen* shown in the preceding photo, or another vehicle in the same unit. The crew has rigged what appears to be a camouflage shelter half over the armor shield and 2 cm gun. The camouflage scheme consists of roughly brushed swatches of a dark color over the vehicle's base color, which probably was *Dunkelgelb* (dark yellow). *Patton Museum*

With the forward portion of the vehicle resembling an Sd.Kfz. 251/1 Ausf. A, and apparently sharing mechanical components with that type as well as the Sd.Kfz. 11 3-ton semitrack, this vehicle mounts an imposing-looking weapon, the 7.5 cm PaK 42 L/70. This weapon, originally intended for use on a field carriage, was experimentally tested on this half-truck chassis. Ultimately the weapon was redesignated KwK 42 and were mounted on Panther tanks. *Patton Museum*

Like so many weapons developed by the Reich, the high-velocity, 75 mm armed, 3-ton half-track did not enter production, but it elicited the interest of the highest echelon of the military, as evidenced by the presence of Adolf Hitler in the admiring crowd. *Patton Museum*

Regardless of the specific origin of the chassis used for this mounting, there is a little doubt that the weight and recoil of the powerful antitank gun would overwhelm capacity of a nominal 3-ton rating of the chassis. Nevertheless, the resulting vehicle was an interesting union of largely standard components. *Patton Museum*

An Sd.Kfz. 251/10, an armored personnel carrier armed with a 3.7 cm PaK, crawls onto an improvised ferry near Kharkov in May 1942. The vehicle is painted in panzer gray and displays a *Balkenkreuz* on the upper armor of the rear compartment. *BA 169-0422*

Specifications Sd.Kfz. 251/1 Ausf. D	
Length	5.80 meters
Width	2.1 meters
Height	2.1 meters
Weight	8.5 tons
Fuel capacity	160 liters
Maximum speed	53 km/hr.
Range, on road	300 km
Range, cross-country	150 km
Crew	2
Communications	FuG Spr Ger f
Engine make	Maybach
Engine model	HL42 TUKRRM
Engine configuration	6-cylinder, liquid cooled
Engine displacement	4.170 liters
Engine horsepower	100 @ 2,800 rpm